In my formative years as a young Christian, I was acutely aware of the fact that I faced many challenges to Christian thinking and behaviour. Few writers helped me to understand how I should respond to these challenges and think and live as a Christian as much as John Stott did. The challenges of faithfulness to God's way are more acute and complex today than when I was a young Christian. In these little books, you find the essence of Stott's thinking about the Christian life; it is refreshing to read this material again and see how relevant and health-giving it is for today. I'm grateful to Inter-Varsity Press and to Tim Chester for making Stott's thinking accessible to a new generation.

Ajith Fernando, Teaching Director, Youth for Christ, Sri Lanka

Technology has enabled more voices to clamour for our attention than ever before, while, at the same time, people's ability to listen carefully seems to have deteriorated as never before. John Stott's speaking and writing was renowned for two things in particular: he taught us how to listen attentively to God in order to live faithfully for God; and he modelled how to listen to the world sensitively in order to communicate God's purposes intelligibly. He taught us to listen. That is why it is such a thrill to see *The Contemporary Christian* carefully revived in a new format as a series for a new generation of readers. As we read, may we li ·

Mark Meynell ~~~~~~~~~~~ ~ean) Langham
Preaching ~~~~~~~~~~~~~~~~ of *Cross-Examined*
and *When* ~~~~~~~~~~~~

It is always ~~~~~~~~~~~~~~~~~ ...ng and challenging reading from the pen of Jc ~~~ ~..ott. I am totally delighted that one of his most significant works will continue to be available, hopefully for more decades to come. The way Stott strives to be faithful to the Word of God and relevant to his world – secularized Western society – as the locus for the drama of God's action, is exemplary, especially for those of us ordained to the service of the church in our diverse contexts. I highly commend The Contemporary Christian series to all who share the same pursuit – listening intently to God's Word and God's world, hearing and obeying God.

David Zac Niringiye, author of *The Church: God's Pilgrim People*

I am delighted that a new generation will now be able to benefit from this rich teaching, which so helped me when it first appeared. As always with John Stott, there is a wonderful blend of faithful exposition of the Bible, rigorous engagement with the world and challenging applications for our lives.

Vaughan Roberts, Rector, St Ebbe's Church, Oxford, and author of a number of books, including *God's Big Picture* (IVP)

Imagine being like a child overwhelmed by hundreds of jigsaw puzzle pieces – you just can't put them together! And then imagine that a kindly old uncle comes along and helps you to assemble the whole thing, piece by piece. That is what it felt like reading John Stott's book *The Contemporary Christian*. For those of us who feel we can't get our heads around our Bibles, let alone our world, he comes along and, with his staggering gifts of clarity and insight, helps us, step by step, to work out what it means to understand our world through biblical lenses. It's then a great blessing to have Tim Chester's questions at the end of each chapter, which help us to think through and internalize each step.

Rico Tice, Senior Minister for Evangelism, All Souls, Langham Place, London, and co-author of *Christianity Explored*

I have long benefited from the work of John Stott because of the way he combines rigorous engagement of the biblical text and careful engagement with the culture of his day. The Contemporary Christian series presents Stott at his very best. It displays his commitment to biblical authority, his zeal for the mission of the church and his call to faithful witness in the world. Stott's reflections here are a must-read for church leaders today.

Trevin Wax, Director of Bibles and Reference, LifeWay Christian Resources, and author of *This Is Our Time* and *Eschatological Discipleship*

All the royalties from this book have been irrevocably assigned to Langham Literature. Langham Literature is a ministry of Langham Partnership, founded by John Stott. Chris Wright is the International Ministries Director.

Langham Literature provides Majority World preachers, scholars and seminary libraries with evangelical books and electronic resources through publishing and distribution, grants and discounts. They also foster the creation of indigenous evangelical books in many languages through writers' grants, strengthening local evangelical publishing houses and investment in major regional literature projects.

For further information on Langham Literature, and the rest of Langham Partnership, visit the website at <www.langham.org>.

The Contemporary Christian

THE WORLD

A Mission to Be Accomplished

John Stott with Tim Chester

INTER-VARSITY PRESS
36 Causton Street, London SW1P 4ST, England
Email: ivp@ivpbooks.com
Website: www.ivpbooks.com

This volume has been adapted from John Stott, *The Contemporary Christian* (1992), and is one of five titles published in this format in The Contemporary Christian series, with extra text, including questions, by Tim Chester.

British Library Cataloguing-in-Publication Data
A catalogue record for this book is available from the British Library.

ISBN: 978–1–78359–926–4
eBook ISBN: 978–1–78359–927–1

Set in Minion

Typeset in Great Britain by CRB Associates, Potterhanworth, Lincolnshire
Print and production managed in Great Britain by Jellyfish Print Solutions

Inter-Varsity Press publishes Christian books that are true to the Bible and that communicate the gospel, develop discipleship and strengthen the church for its mission in the world.

IVP originated within the Inter-Varsity Fellowship, now the Universities and Colleges Christian Fellowship, a student movement connecting Christian Unions in universities and colleges throughout Great Britain, and a member movement of the International Fellowship of Evangelical Students. Website: www.uccf.org.uk. That historic association is maintained, and all senior IVP staff and committee members subscribe to the UCCF Basis of Faith.

Contents

About the authors

John Stott had a worldwide ministry as a church leader, a Bible expositor and the author of many award-winning books. He was Rector Emeritus of All Souls, Langham Place, London, and Founder-President of the Langham Partnership.

Tim Chester is Pastor of Grace Church, Boroughbridge, North Yorkshire, Chair of Keswick Ministries and the author of more than forty books.

Preface

To be 'contemporary' is to live in the present, and to move with the times without worrying too much about the past or the future.

To be a 'contemporary Christian', however, is to live in a present which is enriched by our knowledge of the past and by our expectation of the future. Our Christian faith demands this. Why? Because the God we trust and worship is 'the Alpha and the Omega . . . who is, and who was, and who is to come, the Almighty',[1] while the Jesus Christ we follow is 'the same yesterday and today and for ever'.[2]

So this book and series are about how Christians handle time – how we can bring the past, the present and the future together in our thinking and living. Two main challenges face us. The first is the tension between the 'then' (past) and the 'now' (present), and the second the tension between the 'now' (present) and the 'not yet' (future).

The Introduction opens up the first problem. Is it possible for us truly to honour the past and live in the present at the same time? Can we preserve Christianity's historic identity intact without cutting ourselves off from those around us? Can we communicate the gospel in ways that are exciting and modern without distorting or even destroying it? Can we be authentic and fresh at the same time, or do we have to choose?

The Conclusion opens up the second problem: the tension between the 'now' and the 'not yet'. How far can we explore and experience everything that God has said and done through Christ without straying into what has not yet been revealed or given? How can we develop a proper sense of humility about a future yet to unfold without becoming complacent about where we are in the present?

In between these enquiries into the influences of the past and the future comes an exploration about our Christian responsibilities in the present.

This series is about questions of doctrine and discipleship under the five headings: 'The Gospel', 'The Disciple', 'The Bible', 'The Church' and 'The World' (the book you are holding in your hands), though I make no attempt to be systematic, let alone exhaustive.

In addition to the topic of time, and the relations between past, present and future, there is a second theme running through this series: the need for us to talk less and listen more.

I believe we are called to the difficult and even painful task of 'double listening'. We are to listen carefully (although of course with differing degrees of respect) both to the ancient Word and to the modern world, in order to relate the one to the other with a combination of faithfulness and sensitivity.

Each book in this series is an attempt at double listening. It is my firm conviction that, if we can only develop our capacity for double listening, we will avoid the opposite pitfalls of unfaithfulness and irrelevance, and truly be able to speak God's Word to God's world with effectiveness today.

Adapted from the original Preface by John Stott in 1991

A note to the reader

The original book entitled *The Contemporary Christian*, on which this volume and series are based, may not seem 'contemporary' to readers more than a quarter of a century later. But both the publisher and John Stott's Literary Executors are convinced that the issues which John Stott addresses in this book are every bit as relevant today as when they were first written.

The question was how to make this seminal work accessible for new generations of readers. We have sought to do this in the following ways:

- The original work has been divided into a series of several smaller volumes based on the five major sections of the original.
- Words that may not resonate with the twenty-first-century reader have been updated, while great care has been taken to maintain the thought process and style of the author in the original.
- Each chapter is now followed by questions from a current bestselling Christian author to aid reflection and response.

Lovers of the original work have expressed delight that this book is being made available in a way that extends its reach and influence well into a new century. We pray that your life will be enriched as you read, as the lives of many have already been greatly enriched by the original edition.

Series introduction
The Contemporary Christian –
the then and the now

The expression 'the contemporary Christian' strikes many as a contradiction in terms. Isn't Christianity an antique relic from the remote past, irrelevant to people in today's world?

My purpose in this series is to show that there is such a thing as 'contemporary Christianity' – not something newfangled, but original, historic, orthodox, biblical Christianity, sensitively related to the modern world.

Christianity: both historical and contemporary

We begin by reaffirming that Christianity is a historical religion. Of course, every religion arose in a particular historical context. Christianity, however, makes an especially strong claim to be historical because it rests not only on a historical *person*, Jesus of Nazareth, but on certain historical *events* which involved him, especially his birth, death and resurrection. There is a common thread here with the Judaism from which Christianity sprang. The Old Testament presents God not only as 'the God of Abraham, Isaac and Jacob', but also as the God of the covenant which he made with Abraham, and then renewed with Isaac and Jacob. Again, he is not only 'the God of Moses', but is also seen as the Redeemer responsible for the exodus, who went on to renew the covenant yet again at Mount Sinai.

Christians are forever tethered in heart and mind to these decisive, historical events of the past. We are constantly encouraged in the

1

Bible to look back to them with thankfulness. Indeed, God deliberately made provision for his people to recall his saving actions on a regular basis. Supremely, the Lord's Supper or Holy Communion enables us to call the atoning death of Christ regularly to mind, and so bring the past into the present.

But the problem is that Christianity's foundational events took place such a long time ago. I had a conversation with two brothers some years ago – students who told me they had turned away from the faith of their parents. One was now an agnostic, the other an atheist. I asked why. Did they no longer believe in the truth of Christianity? No, their dilemma was not whether Christianity was *true*, but whether it was *relevant*. How could it be? Christianity, they went on, was a primitive, Palestinian religion from long ago. So what on earth did it have to offer them, living in the exciting modern world?

This view of Christianity is widespread. The world has changed dramatically since Jesus' day, and goes on changing with ever more bewildering speed. People reject the gospel, not necessarily because they think it false, but because it no longer resonates with them.

In response to this we need to be clear about the basic Christian conviction that God continues to speak through what he has spoken. His Word is not a prehistoric fossil, but a living message for the contemporary world. Even granted the historical particularities of the Bible and the immense complexities of the modern world, there is still a fundamental correspondence between them. God's Word remains a lamp to our feet and a light for our path.[1]

At the same time, our dilemma remains. Can Christianity both retain its authentic identity *and* demonstrate its relevance?

The desire to present Jesus in a way that appeals to our own generation is obviously right. This was the preoccupation of the German pastor Dietrich Bonhoeffer while in prison during World War 2: 'What is bothering me incessantly,' he wrote, 'is the question . . . who Christ really is for us today?'[2] It is a difficult question. In answering it, the church has tended in every generation to develop images of Christ which deviate from the portrait painted by the New Testament authors.

Attempting to modernize Jesus

Here are some of the church's many attempts to present a contemporary picture of Christ, some of which have been more successful than others in remaining loyal to the original.

I think first of *Jesus the ascetic* who inspired generations of monks and hermits. He was much like John the Baptist, for he too dressed in a camel's hair cloak, wore sandals or went barefoot, and munched locusts with evident relish. But it would be hard to reconcile this portrait with his contemporaries' criticism that he was a party-goer who 'came eating and drinking'.[3]

Then there was *Jesus the pale Galilean*. The apostate emperor Julian tried to reinstate Rome's pagan gods after Constantine had replaced them with the worship of Christ, and is reported as having said on his deathbed in AD 363, 'You have conquered, O Galilean.' His words were popularized by the nineteenth-century poet Swinburne:

Thou hast conquered, O pale Galilean;
The world has grown grey from thy breath.

This image of Jesus was perpetuated in medieval art and stained glass, with a heavenly halo and a colourless complexion, eyes lifted to the sky and feet never quite touching the ground.

In contrast to the presentations of Jesus as weak, suffering and defeated, there was *Jesus the cosmic Christ*, much loved by the Byzantine church leaders. They depicted him as the King of kings and Lord of lords, the creator and ruler of the universe. Yet, exalted high above all things, glorified and reigning, he seemed aloof from the real world, and even from his own humanity, as revealed in the incarnation and the cross.

At the opposite end of the theological spectrum, the seventeenth- and eighteenth-century deists of the Enlightenment constructed in their own image *Jesus the teacher of common sense*,[4] entirely human and not divine at all. The most dramatic example is the work of Thomas Jefferson, President of the United States from 1801 to 1809. Rejecting the supernatural as incompatible with reason, he produced his own edition of the Gospels, in which all miracles and mysteries were systematically eliminated. What is left is a guide to a merely human moral teacher.

In the twentieth century we were presented with a wide range of options. Two of the best known owe their popularity to musicals. There is *Jesus the clown* of *Godspell*, who spends his time singing and dancing, and thus captures something of the gaiety of Jesus, but hardly takes his mission seriously. Somewhat similar is *Jesus Christ Superstar*, the disillusioned celebrity who once thought he knew who he was, but in Gethsemane was no longer sure.

The late President of Cuba, Fidel Castro, frequently referred to Jesus as 'a great revolutionary', and there have been many attempts to portray him as *Jesus the freedom fighter*, the urban guerrilla, the first-century Che Guevara, with black beard and flashing eyes, whose most characteristic gesture was to overthrow the tables of the moneychangers and to drive them out of the temple with a whip.

These different portraits illustrate the recurring tendency to update Christ in line with current fashions. It began in the apostolic age, with Paul needing to warn of false teachers who were preaching 'a Jesus other than the Jesus we [apostles] preached'.[5] Each succeeding generation tends to read back into him its own ideas and hopes, and create him in its own image.

Their motive is right (to paint a contemporary portrait of Jesus), but the result is always distorted (as the portrait is unauthentic). The challenge before us is to present Jesus to our generation in ways that are both accurate and appealing.

Calling for double listening

The main reason for every betrayal of the authentic Jesus is that we pay too much attention to contemporary trends and too little to God's Word. The thirst for relevance becomes so demanding that we feel we have to give in to it, whatever the cost. We become slaves to the latest fad, prepared to sacrifice truth on the altar of modernity. The quest for relevance degenerates into a lust for popularity. For the opposite extreme to irrelevance is accommodation, a feeble-minded, unprincipled surrender to the spirit of the time.

God's people live in a world which can be actively hostile. We are constantly exposed to the pressure to conform.

Thank God, however, that there have always been those who have stood firm, sometimes alone, and refused to compromise. I think of Jeremiah in the sixth century BC, and Paul in his day ('everyone . . . has deserted me'),[6] Athanasius in the fourth century and Luther in the sixteenth.

In our own day we too need to resolve to present the biblical gospel in such a way as to speak to modern dilemmas, fears and frustrations, but with equal determination not to compromise it in so doing. Some stumbling-blocks are intrinsic to the original gospel and cannot be eliminated or soft-pedalled in order to make it easier to accept. The gospel contains some features so alien to modern thought that it will always appear foolish, however hard we strive to show that it is 'true and reasonable'.[7] The cross will always be an assault on human self-righteousness and a challenge to human self-indulgence. Its 'scandal' (stumbling-block) simply cannot be removed. The church speaks most authentically not when it has become indistinguishable from the world around us, but when its distinctive light shines most brightly.

However keen we are to communicate God's Word to others, we must be faithful to that Word and, if necessary, be prepared to suffer for it. God's word to Ezekiel encourages us: 'Do not be afraid of them . . . You must speak my words to them, whether they listen or fail to listen, for they are rebellious.'[8] Our calling is to be faithful and relevant, not merely trendy.

How, then, can we develop a Christian mind which is both shaped by the truths of historic, biblical Christianity and also fully immersed in the realities of the contemporary world? We have to begin with a double refusal. We refuse to become either so absorbed in the Word that we *escape* into it and fail to let it confront the world, or so absorbed in the world that we *conform* to it and fail to subject it to the judgment of the Word.

In place of this double refusal, we are called to double listening. We need to listen to the Word of God with expectancy and humility, ready for God perhaps to confront us with a word that may be disturbing and uninvited. And we must also listen to the world around us. The voices we hear may take the form of shrill and strident protest. There will also be the anguished cries of those who are suffering, and the pain, doubt, anger, alienation and even despair of those who are at odds with God. We listen to the Word with humble reverence, anxious to understand it, and resolved to believe and obey what we come to understand. We listen to the world with critical alertness, anxious to understand it too, and resolved not necessarily to believe and obey it, but to sympathize with it and to seek grace to discover how the gospel relates to it.

Everybody finds listening difficult. But are Christians sometimes less good at listening than others? We can learn from the so-called 'comforters' in the Old Testament book of Job. They began well. When they heard about Job's troubles, they came to visit him and, seeing how great his sufferings were, said nothing to him for a whole week. If only they had continued as they began, and kept their mouths shut! Instead, they trotted out their conventional view – that every sinner suffers for his or her own sins – in the most insensitive way. They did not really listen to what Job had to say. They merely repeated their own thoughtless and heartless claptrap, until in the end God stepped in and rebuked them for having misrepresented him.

We need to cultivate 'double listening', the ability to listen to two voices at the same time – the voice of God through the Bible and the voices of men and women around us. These voices will often contradict one another, but our purpose in listening to them both is to discover how they relate to each other. Double listening is indispensable to Christian discipleship and to Christian mission.

It is only through this discipline of double listening that it is possible to become a 'contemporary Christian'. We bring 'historical' and 'contemporary' together as we learn to apply the Word to the world, proclaiming good news which is both true and new.

To put it in a nutshell, we live in the 'now' in the light of the 'then'.

The World
Introduction

In theory, the world is the old and fallen community, while the church is God's new and redeemed society. Some theologians, keen to minimize the difference, go so far as to identify them by applying to all human beings indiscriminately the label 'the people of God'. Others reach the same goal by a different route. They allow the world to dictate to the church what its views and values should be, until the church conforms to the world and the two become virtually indistinguishable. A third group is content for the church and the world to live together in amicable co-existence, with neither invading the other's territory or interfering in the other's affairs.

A fourth possibility, however, is what Jesus and his apostles envisaged. It is that the church has a God-given responsibility to infiltrate the world, listening to its challenges, but also bringing its own challenge by sharing the good news in word and deed. The correct term for this task is 'mission'. 'Mission' is what God sends the church into the world to do. We are going to consider four major aspects of it.

In chapter 1, we look at the uniqueness of Jesus Christ, arguably the most important and the most urgent issue before the worldwide church today. Can we still apply traditional words like 'unique', 'absolute' and 'final' to Jesus? Or must we surrender to the pressures of 'pluralism', which insists that Jesus was only one of a number of religious leaders, and that every religion has its own independent validity? If Jesus was and is unique in his person and work, then we are under obligation to make him known. If he is not, then the chief foundation of the Christian mission has been undermined, and we will have to give up our ambition to win the world for Christ.

In chapter 2, we will set out the full biblical basis for the Christian mission. This goes beyond the uniqueness of Christ to the nature of God himself. For mission begins in the heart of God. The living God of the biblical revelation is a missionary God. A rapid survey of the whole of Scripture will demonstrate that each of its five sections has an unavoidably missionary emphasis.

In chapter 3, 'Holistic mission', we will see that the church's communication of the gospel cannot only be in words, but must also be in works. In the church's mission, as in Christ's, good news and good deeds go together.[1] In God's purposes, evangelism and social responsibility are married, and they must not be divorced.

In chapter 4, we will return to Christ, since nothing is more important in the Christian mission than a clear and fresh vision of him. Under the title 'The Christology of mission', we will look at the five main events in the saving career of Jesus in order to see that each has a missionary dimension. From them, we will learn the model, costliness, mandate, motivation and urgency of the mission to which we are called.

1

The uniqueness of Jesus Christ

A social worker in Nigeria once visited a young man in one of the back streets of Lagos. Beside his bed he found the Bible, the Book of Common Prayer, the Qur'an, three copies of *Watchtower* (the magazine of the Jehovah's Witnesses), a biography of Karl Marx, a book of yoga exercises and – what the poor fellow evidently needed most – a popular paperback entitled *How to Stop Worrying*.[1]

In 1966 the first multi-faith service was held in the church of St Martin-in-the-Fields in London. Hindus, Buddhists, Muslims and Christians took part on equal terms, making four affirmations of a supposedly common faith, giving four readings from their respective sacred scriptures, and pronouncing four blessings. In only one of these blessings was the name of Jesus mentioned for the first and last time. The secular press was enthusiastic, hailing it as 'a significant milestone in religious history'. But the Christian newspapers described it as 'a betrayal of the Christian faith'. It is doubtful if they would write anything similar today, for multi-faith services are held regularly.

These two incidents, the one in Lagos and the other in London, are examples of the spirit of syncretism. Dr Visser 't Hooft, the first General Secretary of the World Council of Churches, defined syncretism as the view 'that there is no unique revelation in history, that there are many different ways to reach the divine reality, that all formulations of religious truth or experience are by their very nature inadequate expressions of that truth, and that it is necessary to harmonize as much as possible all religious ideas and experiences so as to create one universal religion for mankind'.[2] He was outspoken in his rejection of this outlook. 'It is high time that Christians should rediscover,' he went on, 'that the very heart of their faith is that Jesus Christ did not come to make a contribution to the religious storehouse of mankind, but that in him God reconciled the world unto himself.'[3]

Today the main challenge to the traditional understanding of the uniqueness of Christ is not 'syncretism', but 'pluralism', not the attempt to fuse the world's religions into a single, universal faith, but the recognition of the integrity of each in all its distinctive diversity.

The options before us are now usually summarized as 'exclusivism', 'inclusivism' and 'pluralism'.[4]

'Exclusivism' (an unfortunately negative term, which gives the impression of wanting to exclude people from the kingdom of God) is used to denote the historic Christian view that salvation cannot be found in other religions, but only in Jesus Christ.

'Inclusivism' allows that salvation is possible to adherents of other faiths, but says this salvation is due to the secret and often unrecognized work of Christ. At the Vatican II Council, Roman Catholics embraced this view, stating that Christ's saving work holds good 'not only for Christians, but for all men of good will in whose hearts grace works in an unseen way'.[5]

'Pluralism' goes further still. Its advocates rejecting exclusivism as 'presumptuous' and 'arrogant', and inclusivism as 'patronizing' or 'condescending'. Whereas 'plurality' expresses the simple fact that there are many religions, 'pluralism' affirms their independent validity. It renounces every claim that Christianity is 'absolute', 'unique', 'definitive', 'final', 'normative', 'ultimate' or 'universal'. 'Unlimited growth is cancer, and so would be an ever-growing single Christian religion all over the world.'[6] Instead, Christianity must be viewed as only one religion among many, and Jesus as only one saviour among others. This is the so-called 'deeper and larger ecumenism that embraces the whole of humanity', of which the rainbow remains 'a timeless symbol'.[7]

Arguments for pluralism

What is it about 'pluralism' that many find attractive?

First, there is *a global consciousness.* Threats to the natural environment, fears of a nuclear conflict and the continuing economic injustice between North and South have led to a planetary perspective. The very survival of the human race seems to depend on learning to live together in harmony and to cooperate for the common good. Whatever divides us, therefore, including our religions, is understandably regarded with increasing disfavour.

In response, Christians should indeed be in the forefront of seeking global harmony. By God's creation we are one people in the world. We should be committed to international peace-making, democracy, human rights, community relations, environmental responsibility and the search for a new international economic order. Moreover, people of different races and religions can, should and do cooperate in these kinds of social action. In order to do so, however, it is not necessary to renounce our belief in the uniqueness of Jesus Christ. It would be folly to seek unity at the expense of truth, or reconciliation without Christ the mediator. Besides, Christ unavoidably divides people as well as uniting them. He said he had come not 'to bring peace, but a sword'.[8] He envisaged that some conflict would continue, as people ranged themselves for or against him.

Second, there is *an appreciation of other religions.* Modern communications (especially television, travel and the internet) have caused the world to shrink. People of strange beliefs and customs, who previously were very remote from us, now live next door. They enter our homes – if not in person then on the screen. This is 'a newly experienced reality for many today'.[9] The sacred books of other faiths, translated into our languages, are now readily available. And, as we become better acquainted with the world's religions, what Professor John Hick has called their 'immense spiritual riches' have 'tended to erode the plausibility of the old Christian exclusivism'.[10] Furthermore, some ancient faiths are showing signs of resurgence, just when the perception is that Christianity, declining in the West, 'has not succeeded in breaking the power of the great historical religions'.[11]

We should welcome today's more thorough knowledge of world faiths, not least through the comparative study of religions in schools. But if we discover 'riches' in other religions, we will also discern more clearly the absolute uniqueness of Jesus Christ, as we will see later. 'To make exclusive claims for our particular tradition,' writes Stanley Samartha, an advocate of pluralism, 'is not the best way to love our neighbours as ourselves.'[12] But in fact, it is the very best and highest way to express neighbour-love, if the gospel is true. For if the gospel is true, then we cannot claim to love our neighbours if we leave them in ignorance of Christ. As for the vitality of other religions, and the comparative failure of Christianity, these things should lead us not to the conclusion that the gospel is untrue, but rather to self-examination, repentance, change, and the adoption of better ways of sharing the good news with others.

Third, there is *a post-colonial modesty*. For four centuries the West dominated the world in political, military, economic and scientific terms, and took for granted its moral and spiritual superiority. Indeed, Christianity's 'attitude to other religions has been shaped by the colonial mentality'.[13] The end of the Second World War, however, heralded the end of the colonial era. As the West underwent a profound cultural shift 'from a position of clear superiority to one of rough parity', a parallel shift took place in theological conscious-ness. Professor Langdon Gilkey writes, 'This dramatic situation has forced . . . a new understanding of the interrelationships of religions, a new balance of spiritual power, so to speak, on all.' It has pushed us all out of 'superiority' into 'parity'.[14] To continue, therefore, to claim Christian universality, it is said, is to lapse into the old imperialist mindset.

It is certainly embarrassing for us in the West to acknowledge that during those centuries of colonial expansion, territorial and spiritual conquest, politics and religion, gun and Bible, the flag and the cross, too often went hand in hand. Representatives of the imperial power developed attitudes of proud superiority towards those they ruled. But 'superiority' is a slippery word. It can describe an air of intolerable conceit, and we need to repent of every vestige of this. But seeking to win followers of other religions to Christ is not in itself a mark of arrogance. Instead, it indicates a profound and humble conviction that the gospel *is* superior to other faiths because it is God's revealed truth.

The attraction of pluralism is more, however, than a concern for global harmony, an appreciation of other religions and a desire for post-colonial modesty. It has even deeper roots, which the twelve contributors to the 1987 book *The Myth of Christian Uniqueness* examined. These scholars describe themselves as having 'crossed a theological Rubicon', not only from exclusivism to inclusivism, but from inclusivism to pluralism,[15] and they tell us about the three 'bridges' which led them to make the crossing.

The first they call the *historico-cultural* bridge, or *relativity*. Since people began applying Einstein's general theory of relativity beyond physics to other spheres (including religion), seemingly nothing has remained absolute. A historical and comparative study of religions, argues Professor Gordon Kaufman, suggests that they are simply 'creations of the human imagination',[16] each from its particular cultural perspective. So Christian theology must give up any claim to absolute or final truth, and understand itself instead as 'a human imaginative response to the necessity to find orientation for life in a particular historical situation'.[17] Professor Tom Driver goes further, declaring that 'even Scripture . . . is the creation of us human beings'.[18]

Now of course we also affirm that the Bible is a culturally conditioned book in the sense that each of its authors spoke within his own particular culture. But is this emphasis on the human, historical and cultural background of the Bible a complete account of its nature? No. There are good reasons for believing in the dual authorship of Scripture, namely that behind the human authors stood the divine author, who spoke his Word through their words, and that his Word transcends both history and culture. It may be that other religions could be described (whatever their claims may be) as 'products of the human imagination'. But the historic Christian belief is that the gospel is the product of divine revelation, albeit mediated through the minds and mouths of the human authors.

The second 'bridge' across the 'theological Rubicon' is labelled *theologico-mystical*, or *mystery*. That is, there is in every religion some sense of the Transcendent or experience of God who, because he is infinite and ineffable, always remains beyond our apprehensions of him. Professor Wilfred Cantwell Smith says all our theologies are only 'conceptual images of God', and 'like other images, each may be less or more worthy of its Subject'. There is, in principle, he goes on, 'no fundamental difference . . . between a doctrine and a statue'. The former is an intellectual image of God, the latter a visual. 'It is wrong for our intellects to absolutize their own handiwork.' For 'both theology and art proffer relative apprehensions of the Absolute'; to absolutize our image of God is idolatry.[19] He goes further: 'For Christians to think that Christianity is true, or final, or salvific, is a form of idolatry. For Christians to imagine that God has constructed Christianity . . . rather than that He/She/It has inspired us to construct it . . . that is idolatry.'[20] Or, as Tom Driver sums it up, 'Idolatry is the insistence that there is only one way, one norm, one truth.'[21]

In response, we certainly agree that God is the Transcendent Reality beyond all possible human imagination, apprehension or description. Words cannot capture, let alone contain, him. Because he is infinite, we shall never come to the end of him. Instead, we will spend eternity exploring and worshipping his fathomless being. Nevertheless, to say that he remains a mystery is compatible with affirming that he has revealed himself. Moreover, his Word incarnate in Jesus and his Word written in Scripture have a normative position for all Christian believers. It is extraordinary to claim that all Christians of all churches for two millennia, who have believed in the uniqueness of Jesus, are idolaters! If the reference is to 'Christianity' as a human construct, then perhaps to absolutize it could become an idolatry. But to acknowledge the finality and absoluteness of Christ himself is not idolatry, but authentic worship.

Third, there is the *ethico-practical* bridge, or *justice*. Some people argue for pluralism because they believe it will contribute to the pursuit of global justice.[22] Borrowing a number of concepts from liberation theology, Professor Paul Knitter writes that 'a preferential option for the poor and the non-person constitutes the necessity and the primary purpose of inter-religious dialogue'. In other words, pluralism is not an end in itself, but a means to the end of liberating the oppressed. Since this is too big a task for any one religion to accomplish, 'a worldwide liberation movement needs a worldwide inter-religious dialogue'.[23] The only possible criterion by which to judge or 'grade' religions must be neither doctrinal nor mystical, but ethical, namely their effectiveness in promoting human well-being.

We must agree that contemporary issues of social justice should be of enormous concern to all Christians, since we acknowledge the dignity of human beings as people made in God's image. We should therefore be ashamed that evangelical Christians have all too often tended to be in the rearguard, instead of in the vanguard, of social reform. We have no quarrel with the proposal to assess religions, including Christianity, according to their social record, since we claim that the gospel is the power of God to transform both individuals and communities. It is because we have both experienced this power in our own lives and seen it at work in human history that we cannot agree with Professor Hick's negative assessment of the Christian social record as 'a complex mixture of valuable and harmful elements', neither better nor worse than those of other religions.[24]

Summary

Our response to the six reasons why some find pluralism attractive is in each case fundamentally the same. They beg the question of truth. Has God fully and finally revealed himself in Christ and the Bible's testimony to Christ, or not?

1 We agree with the search for global harmony, but not at the expense of truth.
2 We agree that a greater knowledge of other religions is enriching, but in comparing them we cannot surrender Christ's claim to be the truth.
3 We agree that colonial attitudes of superiority were arrogant, but still insist that truth is superior to falsehood.
4 We agree that Scripture is culturally conditioned, but affirm that through it God has spoken his Word of truth.
5 We agree that the ultimate mystery of God is beyond human apprehension, but affirm that God has truly revealed himself in Christ.
6 We agree that it is an essential part of our Christian calling to serve the poor, but we are also called to bear witness to the truth.

According to Professor Rosemary Radford Ruether, 'The idea that Christianity, or even the biblical faiths, have a monopoly on religious truth is an outrageous and absurd religious chauvinism.'[25] If by 'monopoly' she means either that other religions possess no truth, or that Christians keep God's revelation to themselves and do not share it, then we could perhaps agree with her strident words. But if by 'monopoly' she is referring to the belief that God has revealed himself fully and finally in Christ, then this is neither outrageous nor absurd, but humble, wise, sober and considered Christian faith.

It would indeed be arrogant, even 'outrageous', if we were claiming uniqueness or finality for our own fallible opinions and limited experiences. But we are not. As Bishop Lesslie Newbigin put it,

> If, in fact, it is true that almighty God, creator and sustainer of all that exists in heaven and on earth, has – at a known time and place in human history – so humbled himself as to become part of our sinful humanity, and to suffer and die a shameful death to take away our sin, and to rise from the dead as the first-fruit of a new creation, if this is a fact, then to affirm it is not arrogance. To remain quiet about it is treason to our fellow human beings. If it is really true, as it is, that 'the Son of God loved me and gave himself up for me', how can I agree that this amazing act of matchless grace should merely become part of a syllabus for the 'comparative study of religions'?[26]

The uniqueness of Jesus Christ

It is essential to clarify that Christians claim uniqueness and finality only for Christ and not for Christianity in any of its many institutional or cultural forms. I call three witnesses to endorse this statement, who come respectively from Africa, Asia and Europe.

First, Professor John Mbiti of Kenya has written, 'The uniqueness of Christianity is in Jesus Christ.'[27]

My Asian witness is Sadhu Sundar Singh, the Indian Christian mystic and evangelist. Brought up in a Sikh home, he converted to Christ as a teenager, and later became a *sadhu*, an itinerant holy man. Visiting a Hindu college one day, he was asked by an agnostic professor of comparative religion what he had found in Christianity that he had not found in his old religion. 'I have Christ,' he replied. 'Yes, I know,' said the professor a little impatiently. 'But what particular principle or doctrine have you found that you did not have before?' 'The particular thing I have found,' he replied, 'is Christ.'[28]

My European witness is the widely travelled Anglican scholar, Bishop Stephen Neill, who emphasized the centrality of Christ in the debate with pluralism. He wrote, 'The old saying "Christianity is Christ" is almost exactly true. The historical figure of Jesus of Nazareth is the criterion by which every Christian affirmation has to be judged, and in the light of which it stands or falls.'[29] Responding to critics of Christianity, he asked,

> Have our interlocutors ever really looked at Jesus Christ and tried to see him as he is? For, if we take the Gospels seriously . . . Jesus is not in the least like anyone else who has ever lived. The things that he says about God are not the same as the sayings of any other religious teacher. The claims that he makes for himself are not the same as those that have been made on behalf of any other religious teacher. His criticisms of human life and society are far more devastating than those that any other man has ever made. The demands he made on his followers are more searching than those put forward by any other religious teacher.[30]

Our claim, then, is not just that Jesus was one of the great spiritual leaders of the world. It would be hopelessly incongruous to refer to him as 'Jesus the Great' and compare him with Alexander the Great, Charles the Great or Napoleon the Great. Jesus is not 'the Great'; he is the only.[31] He has no peers, no rivals and no successors.

So how did the early Christians think of him? They gave him many names and titles. Often he is plain 'Jesus' or 'Christ', or when his human name and messianic title are combined, 'Jesus (the) Christ'. Often again 'the Lord' is added, whether 'the Lord Jesus' or 'the Lord Christ' or 'the Lord Jesus Christ'. But when his title is spelled out in full, he is 'our Lord and Saviour Jesus Christ'. It comes, for example, at the conclusion of 2 Peter: 'But grow in the grace and knowledge of our Lord and Saviour Jesus Christ.'[32]

Within this designation three distinct affirmations are implied, namely that Jesus is Lord, Jesus is Saviour and Jesus is ours. All three declare him to be unique.

Jesus is Lord

'Lord Jesus' was the earliest of all Christian creeds. It is a witness to the incarnation, since it is an affirmation of the oneness of the human Jesus and the divine Lord. The word *kyrios* was used with a wide variety of meanings. On the one hand, it could be used simply as a courtesy title (like 'Sir') or to designate the owner of property. On the other hand, it was used throughout the classical Greek period to refer to the gods as a way of acknowledging their authority over nature and history. It then came to be used of human rulers, especially the emperor. It was also the regular paraphrase for Yahweh, the Old Testament covenant name for God, by the scholars who put the Hebrew Bible into Greek. The fact that it came to be used in the New Testament of the risen Christ,[33] with the implication that his followers were his slaves committed to worship and obey him, is a clear indication that they acknowledged his deity. It is all the more remarkable that his first Jewish disciples used this term, because they were as fiercely monotheistic as any Muslim is today. They recited the *Shema* daily, confessing that 'the LORD our God, the LORD is one'.[34] Yet, in spite of this, they boldly called Jesus 'Lord', and worshipped him as God.

There is nothing like this in any other religion. The Jews still reject the deity of Jesus, of course. So do Muslims. Misunderstanding the incarnation in grossly physical terms, Muhammad wrote in the Qur'an, 'Allah forbid that he himself should beget a son.'[35]

Early or classical Buddhism had no god and no worship. Divine status and honour were not accorded to the Buddha until around 500 years after his death. So we cannot accept the parallel Professor Hick makes when he writes, 'Buddhology and Christology developed in comparable ways.'[36] He claims each 'came to be thought of' as an incarnation as a result of the religious devotion of his followers. The comparison is inept, however, for Jesus' own contemporaries called him 'Lord', while half a millennium passed before the Buddha was worshipped as God.

Hinduism, it is true, claims a number of *avatars* or divine 'descents' in which the god Vishnu is said to have appeared in Rama, Krishna and others. In the Bhagavad Gita Krishna tells Arjuna that he frequently takes human form: 'I have been born many times . . . Although I am unborn, everlasting, and I am the Lord of all, I come to my realm of nature and through my wondrous power I am born.'[37] Perhaps even more striking was the claim of Ramakrishna, the nineteenth-century Hindu reformer, who spoke of himself as 'the same soul that had been born before as Rama, as Krishna, as Jesus, or as Buddha, born again as Ramakrishna'.[38]

But 'incarnation' is not an apt or accurate rendering of the Sanskrit word *avatar*. Linking them conceals the two fundamental differences between the Hindu and the Christian claims. First, there is the question of *historicity*. Vishnu's *avatars* belong to Hindu mythology. It is of no importance to Hindus whether the *avatars* actually happened or not. Christianity, however, is essentially a historical religion, based on the claim that the incarnation of God in Jesus Christ was an event of history that took place in Palestine when Augustus was emperor of Rome. If its historicity could be disproved, Christianity would be destroyed.

The second difference lies in the *plurality* of the *avatars*. Krishna spoke of his multiple, even 'frequent', rebirths. But 'incarnation' and 'reincarnation' are two fundamentally different concepts. The *avatars* were temporary manifestations or embodiments of Vishnu in human beings. But none involved the actual assumption of humanity by divinity, or is in any way central to Hinduism. The Christian claim, by contrast, is that in Jesus of Nazareth God took human nature to himself once and for all and for ever. We claim that God's incarnation in Jesus was decisive, permanent and unrepeatable, the turning point of human history and the beginning of the new age. Reigning at God's right hand today is precisely 'the man Christ Jesus', still human as well as divine, although now his humanity has been glorified. Having assumed our nature, he has never discarded it, and he never will.

So the first aspect of the uniqueness of Jesus is that he is Lord. He is God's eternal, personal 'Word' or 'Son' who became a human being. As a result, 'In Christ all the fullness of the Deity lives in bodily form.'[39] He is the sovereign ruler of the universe and of the church. It is true that he exercises his rule through humble love, for the Lord became the servant and washed his disciples' feet. Yet our rightful place is on our faces at *his* feet.

Jesus is Saviour

The second affirmation contained in the title of Jesus is that he is Saviour: the divine Lord is the divine Saviour. And, although the vocabulary of salvation is distasteful to many people today, we cannot possibly give it up. For Christianity is in essence a rescue religion. It announces good news of salvation. As the churches have recited for centuries in the Nicene Creed, 'for us and for our salvation he came down from heaven'.

Now 'salvation' is a comprehensive word, embracing all God's redeeming purposes for his alienated creatures. Salvation is freedom, with corresponding negative and positive aspects:

- It is freedom from the just judgment of God on our sins, from our guilt and our guilty conscience, into a new relationship with him in which we become his reconciled, forgiven children, and we know him as our Father.
- It is freedom from the bitter bondage of meaninglessness into a new sense of purpose in God's new society of love, in which the last are first, the poor are rich and the meek are heirs.

- It is freedom from the dark prison of our own self-centredness into a new life of self-fulfilment through self-forgetful service.
- And one day it will include freedom from the futility of pain, decay, death and dissolution into a new world of immortality, beauty and unimaginable joy.

All this – and more! – is 'salvation'.

It was to secure these great blessings that Jesus Christ came into the world, died on the cross and rose again. It was he who took the initiative, not us: 'The Son of Man came to seek and to save the lost.'[40] He likened himself to a shepherd who left the rest of his sheep to go after the one that was lost. Far from abandoning it in the hope that it might bleat and stumble its way home, he risked his own life to search it out.[41] In fact, 'the Good Shepherd' laid down his life for his sheep.[42] Deliberately and voluntarily, Jesus went to the cross to identify himself with us. God in Christ took our place, bore our sins, assumed our guilt, paid our penalty, died our death, in order that we might be forgiven and recreated. And then he was raised from death in a supernatural event, to reverse the human verdict against him, and to vindicate his divine-human person and saving work.

This too is unique. We see his uniqueness not only in his incarnation, but also in his atoning death and historical resurrection. The whole concept of a gracious God, who refused either to condone our sins or to visit them upon us, who instead took the initiative to rescue us, who gave himself to the shame and pain of death on the cross, and who broke the power of death in his resurrection, has no parallel in other faiths. 'If any other religion has anything in the least like the doctrines of incarnation and atonement,' wrote Bishop Stephen Neill, 'I have yet to find it.'[43] But it cannot be found. Emil Brunner was right to refer to 'the self-confident optimism of all non-Christian religion', teaching various forms of self-salvation, whereas in the gospel the whole emphasis is on the gracious 'self-movement' of God towards sinners, and on self-despair as 'the ante-chamber of faith'.[44]

Buddhism sees the human predicament in suffering rather than sin, and in the 'desire' which it sees as the root of suffering. Deliverance comes only through the abolition of desire by self-effort. There is no God and no Saviour. 'Strive without ceasing' were the Buddha's last words to his disciples before he died.

Philosophical Hinduism locates our problem in *maya*, usually understood as the 'illusion' of our space-time experience. Popular Hinduism, on the other hand, teaches the inflexible doctrine of *karma*, retribution through reincarnation. Each person must eat the fruit of his own wrongdoings, in future lives if not in this one. From this endless cycle (*samsara*) of rebirths or reincarnations there is no escape by forgiveness. Escape comes only by that final release called nirvana, involving the extinction of individual being and absorption into impersonal divine reality (Brahman).

Judaism continues, of course, to teach the possibility of forgiveness to the penitent, which the Old Testament promised, but denies both that Jesus is the Messiah and that his sin-bearing death is the only ground on which God can forgive. That painstaking and honest Jewish scholar, C. G. Montefiore, saw the 'greatness and originality' of Jesus in his new attitude to sinners. Instead of avoiding them, he actively sought them out. The rabbis had said that God receives sinners who return to him, but they had not spoken of a divine love which makes the first move to seek and to save them: 'This direct search for, and appeal to, the sinner are new and moving notes of high import and significance. The good shepherd who searches for the lost sheep, and reclaims it and rejoices over it, is a new figure.'[45]

Islam clearly proclaims the mercy of God. Each of the 114 *suras* (chapters) of the Qur'an is introduced by the words, 'In the Name of Allah, the Compassionate, the Merciful'. But it includes no costly historical display of his mercy. And when we probe further, we find that Allah is merciful to the meritorious, to those who pray, give alms and fast in Ramadan. There is no message for sinners who deserve judgment, except that they will receive the judgment they deserve. 'Moreover, that which we ask the Muslim to look for in Jesus is in itself a cause of grave offence to Muslim pride. We suggest – we cannot do otherwise – that he find a Saviour. The Muslim affirms that he has no need of any such thing.'[46]

There can be no doubt that the chief difference between Christianity and the world's religions, and the chief stumbling-block which they find in it, is the cross. It humbles all pride and dashes all hopes of self-salvation. It also speaks of the uncalculating generosity of the love of God in providing this way of salvation. It was here that Toyohiko Kagawa, the Japanese Christian leader, found Christianity's uniqueness:

> I am grateful for Shinto, for Buddhism, and for Confucianism. I owe much to these faiths . . . Yet these three faiths utterly failed to minister to my heart's deepest needs. I was a pilgrim journeying upon a long road that had no turning. I was weary. I was footsore. I wandered through a dark and dismal world where tragedies were thick . . . Buddhism teaches great compassion . . . but since the beginning of time, who has declared, 'this is my blood of the covenant which is poured out for many unto remission of sins'?[47]

Jesus is ours

Jesus Christ's full title is not 'the Lord and Saviour' but '*our* Lord and Saviour'. We must not miss this personal possessive adjective. It is a small word, but highly significant. It indicates that there is a third affirmation hidden in his title, namely *Jesus is ours*.

Already in the Old Testament the possessive adjective 'my' regularly expressed the personal relationship which God's covenant people enjoyed with him, especially when they addressed him in prayer. For example, the psalmists write, 'LORD, my Rock and my Redeemer', 'The LORD is my shepherd', 'The LORD is my light and my salvation . . . the stronghold of my life', 'Truly he is my rock and my salvation; he is my fortress' and 'You, God, are my God, earnestly I seek you.'[48]

In the New Testament what is claimed is a comparable personal relationship with Jesus Christ. Both Paul and Peter give us notable examples. Here is Paul: 'I consider everything a loss because of the surpassing worth of knowing Christ Jesus my Lord.'[49] As for Peter, he claims this intimate relationship not for himself alone, but for his readers too: 'Though you have not seen him [i.e. Christ], you love him; and even though you do not see him now, you believe in him and are filled with an inexpressible and glorious joy.'[50]

Here are claims that Christ is our contemporary. The Jesus who was born into our world, and who lived and died in first-century Palestine, also rose from the dead, is now alive for ever, and is available and accessible to his people. Jesus Christ is not to be relegated, like other religious leaders, to history and the history books. He is not dead and gone, finished or fossilized. He is alive and active. He calls us to follow him, and he offers himself to us as our indwelling and transforming Saviour.

The New Testament often explains that this availability to us is through the Holy Spirit, who is his Spirit.[51] Paul prays that 'he [i.e. the Father] may strengthen you with power through his Spirit in your inner being, so that Christ may dwell in your hearts through faith'.[52] Indeed, the Christian faith is essentially trinitarian. We come to the Father through the Son by the Spirit,[53] and the Father comes to us through the Son by the Spirit.[54]

Once again this is unique. There is nothing comparable to it in the other religions. The Buddhist does not claim to know the Buddha, nor the Confucianist Confucius, nor the Muslim Muhammad, nor the Marxist Karl Marx. Each reveres the founder of his religion or ideology as a teacher of the past. To Christians too

Jesus is a teacher, but, even more, he is our living Lord and Saviour. Phrases claiming this 'recur on page after page of the New Testament, and make clear that it is this intimate and personal relationship of trust, devotion and communion, which is the very heart of the Christian faith'.[55]

Archbishop Coggan drew attention to this when referring to the 164 occurrences of Paul's favourite formula, 'in Christ':

> It is a strange phrase. We can scarcely find a parallel use to it in ordinary life. If, let us say, an intimate friend of Churchill who had spent many years with him and then had given a decade to the writing of his life were talking to us about that great man, he might sum up his relationship to him in a wide variety of ways. He might say that he feared him, or admired him, or revered him, or even loved him. But he never would say, 'I am a man in Churchill'. It would never occur to him to use such a phrase. But Paul was, above everything else, 'a man in Christ'.[56]

Although it is right to emphasize in this way the believer's personal, individual relationship to Christ, indicated by the singular possessive 'my', yet his full title actually includes the *plural* possessive 'our'. For God is calling out a *people* for himself, and the focus of his people's unity is Jesus Christ. It is he who comes and stands among us when we meet to worship. 'I am with you,' he says, even when only two or three gather in his name.[57] And he repeats his promise to us when we go out to make disciples of the nations: 'I am with you always, to the very end of the age.'[58]

Here, then, are three major aspects of the uniqueness of Jesus Christ. He is Lord. He is Saviour. He is ours. For he is 'our Lord and Saviour, Jesus Christ'. Historically speaking, these are allusions to his birth, death and resurrection. Theologically speaking, they refer to the incarnation, the atonement and the risen Lord's gift of the Spirit.

Indeed, because in no other person but the historical Jesus of Nazareth has God become human, lived on earth, died for our sins, conquered death, been exalted to heaven and sent the Holy Spirit, therefore there is no other Saviour. For there is no other person who possesses these qualifications, on the basis of which he alone is competent to save.

It is not enough, therefore, to declare that Jesus is unique in the sense that every human being is unique, as indeed every snowflake is unique, and every blade of grass. Nor can we follow Professor Paul Knitter's claim that the 'one and only' language of the New Testament is 'much like the language a husband would use of his wife . . . "you are the most beautiful woman in the world . . . you are the only woman for me"'.[59] It is poetry, hyperbole, but not literal truth, he claims. Later, Professor Knitter argues that it is 'action language', whose *primary* purpose was neither to define doctrine nor to exclude others, but rather to urge action for Christ in 'total commitment to his vision and way'.[60]

But no. This appeal to different uses of language, although ingenious, is surely special pleading. A careful study of the 'one and only' texts in their context shows they are not purely poetic expressions of faith and love, meant to be taken with a pinch of salt. On the contrary, they are solemn affirmations of truth, which have eternal consequences for our salvation. Moreover, all of them, implicitly if not explicitly, draw their negative conclusion ('no other') from their positive statement (he alone). Thus, it is because only Christ knows the Father that only he can make him known,[61] and it is because he is 'the way and the truth and the life' that nobody can come to the Father except through him.[62] Similarly, it is because the name of Jesus Christ, whom God has raised from the dead, is mighty to save, that there is no other saving name.[63] So too (even in the thoroughgoing syncretism of the Greco-Roman world) 'there is but one God, the Father . . . and there is but one Lord, Jesus Christ'.[64] There is one high priest who offered one sacrifice (of himself) as a sin offering once for all.[65] As a result of his death as a ransom for all, 'there is one God and one mediator between God and mankind, the man Christ Jesus'.[66]

Only one way, only one name, only one God, only one Lord, only one mediator. The claim is exclusive, and the implication inescapable. What is genuinely unique has universal significance and must be universally made known, whereas, to quote Visser 't Hooft again, 'There is no universality if there is no unique event.'[67] Thus uniqueness and universality belong together. It is because God has super-exalted Jesus, and given him the unique name of 'Lord', towering above every other name, that every knee must bow to him. It is because Jesus Christ is the only Saviour that we are required to proclaim him everywhere. The 'inclusivism' of the mission is precisely due to the 'exclusivism' of the mediator. Universal authority over the nations has been given to him. This is why he commissions us to go and disciple the nations.[68]

Two questions

Is there a total discontinuity between Christianity and other religions, so that all truth is contained in it and no truth in them? No. Christians certainly do believe that God has revealed himself in Jesus Christ, as witnessed to in Scripture, in a unique and final way. As a result, in this life God has nothing more to reveal than he has revealed (although of course we have much more to learn). But we are not suggesting that outside the church we consider God inactive and truth absent. Not at all. God sustains all his creatures, and therefore 'is not far from any one of them'. By creation they are his 'offspring', who 'live and move and have [their] being' in him.[69] Also Jesus Christ, as the *logos* of God and the light of mankind,[70] is himself ceaselessly active in the world. Because he is described as 'the true light that gives light to everyone',[71] all beauty, truth and goodness, wherever they are found among human beings, derive from him, whether people know it or not. This is an aspect of God's so-called 'common grace', his love shown to all humanity. It is not, however, his 'saving grace', which he extends to those who humbly cry to him for mercy.

Is there no hope of salvation then for those who belong to other religions, and who may never even have heard of Jesus? Our response to this poignant question needs to combine confidence and agnosticism, what we know (because Scripture plainly teaches it) and what we do not know (because Scripture is either unclear or silent about it).

What we know from Scripture is that there is no possibility of self-salvation. For all human beings, on account of God's general revelation, have some knowledge of God and of goodness; all have failed to live up to their knowledge; and all are therefore guilty before God, and are in the state of 'perishing' (unless God intervenes). This is the argument of Romans 1 – 3. Nobody can achieve salvation by his or her religion, sincerity or philanthropy. Those who claim to be Christians cannot, and nor can anyone else. Cornelius the centurion is not an exception to this rule, as has sometimes been suggested. His story teaches that salvation is available to Gentiles as well as to Jews on the same terms. It does not teach that he attained it by his own righteousness, piety or generosity. On the contrary, he needed to hear and respond to the gospel to receive salvation, life, cleansing and the Holy Spirit.[72] So self-salvation is impossible. We also know that Jesus Christ is the only Saviour (because he alone has the necessary qualifications, as we have seen), and that salvation is by God's grace alone, on the basis of Christ's cross alone, by faith alone.

What we do not know, however, is exactly how much knowledge and understanding of the gospel people need before they can cry to God for mercy and be saved. In the Old Testament, people were certainly justified by grace through faith, even though they had little knowledge of Christ. Perhaps there are others today in a somewhat similar position. They know they are sinful and guilty before God, and that they cannot do anything to win his favour, so in self-despair they call upon the God they dimly perceive to save them. If God does save such, as many evangelical Christians tentatively believe, their salvation is still only by grace, only through Christ, only by faith.

Something else we know is that the final number of God's redeemed people will be actually countless,[73] in final fulfilment of God's promise to Abraham that his posterity (spiritual as well as physical) will be 'as numerous as the stars in the sky and as the sand on the seashore'.[74] In the same vein we seem to be assured by Paul that many more people will be saved than lost, because Christ's work in causing salvation will be more successful than Adam's in causing ruin, and because God's grace in bringing life will overflow 'much more' than Adam's trespass in bringing death.[75]

Although we have solid biblical grounds for cherishing this expectation, we are not told how God will achieve it. But, while we remain agnostic about this, our duty is clear. We are commissioned to preach the gospel and make disciples. It is hard for people to call on one they have not believed in, or to believe in one of whom they have not heard, or to hear if no-one preaches to them.[76] It is much easier for people to believe once they have heard the good news of Christ crucified. It is when they learn from the cross about God's mercy to sinners that they cry, 'God be merciful to *me*, a sinner!' As Paul put it, 'faith comes from hearing the message, and the message is heard through the word of Christ.'[77]

So then, to deny the uniqueness of Christ is to cut the nerve of mission and make it superfluous. To affirm his uniqueness, on the other hand, is to acknowledge the urgency of making him universally known.

Reflection questions from Tim Chester

1 What is your experience of encountering other religions?
How has this shaped the attitudes of your unbelieving friends?
How has it shaped your attitudes?

2 Can we learn from the teaching of other religions?

3 How would you respond to a friend who said, 'To claim Christ is the only way to God is ridiculous and arrogant'?

4 What makes Christianity different from every other religion?

5 How should we evangelize members of other religions?

6 Despite the fact that Stott resolutely rejects 'pluralism', he identifies what makes it attractive so he can engage with it at a deeper level. Apply this approach to another position you reject. Why do its proponents find it attractive? How might this help you engage with them more effectively?

2

Our God is a missionary God

The concept of 'mission' is out of favour in today's world, and hostility to it is growing. Evangelism, missionary zeal, attempts to convert other people, are all rejected as 'incompatible with the spirit of tolerance', 'a gross infringement of individual liberties' and 'a most distasteful form of arrogance'. Even in the church some people are indifferent to the church's mission, while others are actively resistant to it.

'How can one religion claim a monopoly of truth?' people ask. 'Are there not many different ways to God?' 'What right have we to interfere in other people's privacy, or attempt to impose our views on them? Let's mind our own business, and hope other people will mind theirs.'

Half-hidden in this negative rhetoric lie three objections to the Christian mission, namely that it is guilty of intolerance, arrogance and violence.

How should we respond to these criticisms?

Intolerant?

Tolerance is perhaps the most prized virtue in Western culture today. But people do not always define what they mean by it. There are three different kinds of tolerance. The first may be called *legal* tolerance. This seeks to ensure that every minority's religious rights (usually summarized as the freedom to 'profess, practise and propagate' religion) are protected in law. Christians should be in the forefront of those demanding this. Another kind is *social* tolerance. This encourages respect for all persons, whatever views they may hold. It seeks to understand and appreciate their position, and promotes good neighbourliness. This too is a virtue that Christians want to cultivate. It arises naturally from our recognition that all human beings are God's creation and bear his image. He wants us to live together in friendship. But what about *intellectual* tolerance, which is the third kind? To cultivate a mind so broad that it can accommodate every opinion, however false or evil, without ever detecting anything to reject, is not a virtue. In fact, it is the vice of the feeble-minded and amoral. It ends up in an unprincipled confusion of truth with error and goodness with evil. Christians who believe that truth and goodness have been revealed in Christ cannot possibly go along with this kind of tolerance. We are resolved to bear witness to Christ, who is the embodiment of both. It was this conviction that led Archbishop William Temple to say, 'Christianity is, I am persuaded, a profoundly intolerant religion.'[1]

Arrogant?

If mission is not in the wrong sense intolerant, is it arrogant? I think we should begin by agreeing that some Christian attitudes and evangelistic methods could justly be described as 'proud' and 'patronizing'. We need to repent of these failings. Evangelists should never be imperialists, ambitious for the growth of their personal empire or for the prestige of their organization rather than the growth and prestige of the kingdom of God. A crusading spirit, a triumphalist mindset and a swashbuckling style are all inappropriate in Christ's ambassadors. Humility is the pre-eminent Christian virtue and should characterize all our thoughts, words and deeds.

Some Western missionaries have made the mistake of confusing Christ with culture. They have then become 'guilty of a cultural imperialism which both undermines the local culture unnecessarily and seeks to impose an alien culture instead'.[2] *The Willowbank Report: Gospel and Culture* puts it like this:

We know we should never condemn or despise another culture, but rather respect it. We advocate neither the arrogance which imposes our culture on others, nor the syncretism which mixes the gospel with cultural elements incompatible with it, but rather a humble sharing of the good news – made possible by the mutual respect of a genuine friendship.[3]

Given this need to repent of personal and cultural arrogance, is the very concept of mission inherently arrogant? Bishop Kenneth Cragg argues that the opposite is the case:

The description of mission as religious egoism may have some validity in relation to some of its disloyalties. But it is finally the abeyance of mission which would be the supremely damnable egoism, for it would argue a proprietary right in that which is too big to belong to a few and too inclusive to be arrogated to some alone ... To believe in Christ at all is to acknowledge him a universal Christ. Because he is requisite for all, he is perquisite to none. The Christian mission is simply an active recognition of the dimensions of the love of God.[4]

Violent?

The third objection to the Christian mission is that it is a violent assault on people. Evangelism seems to them both aggressive and intrusive, involving an unwelcome invasion of private territory. Again we have to acknowledge that this is sometimes true. The Great Commission gives us no warrant to encroach on other people's personal space or crash the barriers with which they seek to protect themselves. Personally, I wish we could purge our evangelistic vocabulary of violent metaphors. 'Crusades' are too reminiscent of medieval military expeditions to the Holy Land, 'campaigns' of army operations, and even 'missions' of wartime bombing raids, while talk of 'targeting' communities is more suggestive of bombs and bullets than of the gospel of peace. How can we evangelize with integrity if we do not display the 'humility and gentleness' of the Christ we proclaim?[5]

When people talk disparagingly of 'proselytism', they generally have in mind some kind of conversion by force. This must be sharply distinguished from true evangelism. Indeed, there is a broad measure of agreement among churches that 'proselytism' is a synonym for 'unworthy witness'.[6] The 'unworthiness' of a proselytizing witness may refer to

- our motives – concern for our own glory, instead of the glory of Christ;
- our methods – trust in psychological pressure techniques or in the offer of benefits on condition of conversion, instead of in the power of the Holy Spirit;
- our message – focusing on the alleged falsehood and failures of others, instead of on the truth and perfection of Jesus Christ.

There is no need to resort to any kind of 'unworthy witness'. For truth is going to prevail in the end. As Paul put it, 'We cannot do anything against the truth, but only for the truth.'[7] Those who use improper pressures are thereby admitting the weakness of their own case.

Authentic Christian mission, then, is fully compatible with a true tolerance, a genuine humility and a Christlike gentleness. It is also integral to historic Christianity. Christianity without mission is no longer Christianity. This is partly, as we saw in the last chapter, because Christianity affirms both the finality of Christ (he has no successors) and the uniqueness of Christ (he has no rivals). His uniqueness gives him universal significance. He must be made known throughout the world.

More than that, Christian mission is rooted in the nature of God himself. The Bible reveals Father, Son and Holy Spirit as a missionary God, who creates a missionary people, and is working towards a missionary consummation. If this chapter were a sermon, I would have to announce my text as being the whole Bible! It would not be possible to select a shorter one, not if we are to lay an adequate biblical foundation for the Christian mission.

I propose, therefore, to present a short overview of the Bible, dividing it into its five main sections. We shall look at

- the Old Testament and God the Father, the Creator of the world and the covenant God of Israel;
- the Gospels and our Lord Jesus Christ, the Saviour of sinners;
- the book of Acts and the Holy Spirit at work in and through the apostles;
- the Letters and the church they depict, living and witnessing responsibly in the world;
- the book of Revelation and the climax of history when the redeemed people of God will be gathered from all nations.

Each successive stage is a fresh missionary disclosure.

The God of the Old Testament is a missionary God

The idea that the Old Testament is a missionary book, and that its God is a missionary God, comes as a surprise to many people. For they have always thought of the God of the Old Testament as exclusively the God of Israel. They remember

- how he called Abraham, and made a covenant with him and his descendants;
- how he renewed his covenant with Isaac and Jacob, and then with the twelve tribes whom he rescued from slavery in Egypt and brought to Mount Sinai, where he promised to be their God and to make them his people;

- how he settled them in the Promised Land and blessed them with kings, priests and prophets, preparing them for the coming of the Messiah.

All this is true. But it is only a part of the truth. For the Old Testament begins

- not with Abraham, but with Adam;
- not with the covenant, but with the creation;
- not with the chosen race, but with the human race.

It declares emphatically that Yahweh, the God of Israel, was not a petty tribal godling like Chemosh, the god of the Moabites, or Milcom, the god of the Ammonites, but the Creator of heaven and earth, the Lord of the nations and 'the God of the spirits of all flesh'.[8] That is its perspective throughout.

The call of Abraham did not contradict this worldview; it established it. Yahweh told Abraham to leave his country, people and household for another land. Then God said to him,

I will make you into a great nation
and I will bless you;
I will make your name great,
and you will be a blessing.
I will bless those who bless you,
and whoever curses you I will curse;
and all peoples on earth
will be blessed through you.[9]

Abraham was to leave his own people and be made into another. God promised not only to bless him, but to make him a blessing; not only to give him a family, but through it to bless 'all peoples on earth'.

It is no exaggeration to say that Genesis 12:1–4 is the most unifying text of the whole Bible. For God's saving purpose to bless the whole world through Christ, who was Abraham's seed, is encapsulated here. The rest of the Bible is an unfolding of this text, and subsequent history has been its fulfilment. For God first prepared Israel for Christ's coming, and then through Christ's coming God has been blessing the world ever since. We ourselves would not be followers of Jesus today if it were not for this text: we are beneficiaries of the promise God made to Abraham about 4,000 years ago. 'If you belong to Christ,' Paul wrote, 'then you are Abraham's seed, and heirs according to the promise.'[10] Again, if we share his faith, 'he is the father of us all'.[11] For God's promise was an advance announcement to Abraham of the gospel, namely that he was going to 'justify the Gentiles by faith'.[12]

The tragedy of the Old Testament is that Israel kept forgetting the universal scope of God's promise. They overlooked the fact that God had chosen one family to bless all families. They became preoccupied with themselves and their own history. They even perverted the truth of God's election into the error of divine favouritism, which led them to boast of their privileged status and assume they were immune to God's judgment.

So the prophets had to keep broadening their outlook, and reminding them that God's purpose through Abraham's descendants was to bless the nations. For example, God would make the *nations* the Messiah's 'inheritance' and 'possession';[13] *all nations* would serve him;[14] he would be a light for the Gentile *nations*;[15] and in that day *all nations* would stream to the mountain of the Lord's temple.[16]

The Christ of the Gospels
is a missionary Christ

In 1850 David Livingstone, the intrepid pioneer missionary in Africa, wrote to his sister Agnes,

Forbid it that we should ever consider the holding of a commission from the King of kings a sacrifice, so long as other
men esteem the service of an earthly government an honour
. . . I am a missionary heart and soul. God had an only son, and
he was a missionary and a physician. A poor, poor imitation of
him I am . . . In this service I hope to live; in it I wish to die.[17]

A few years later Robert Speer, travelling secretary of the Student
Volunteer Movement in the United States, wrote in his journal, 'If
you want to follow Jesus Christ, you must follow him to the ends of
the earth, for that is where he is going . . . We cannot think of God
without thinking of him as a missionary God.'

It is true that Matthew twice describes Jesus restricting his mission
to 'the lost sheep of Israel'. He told the Twelve not to evangelize
Gentile or Samaritan areas, but to 'go rather' to Israel's lost sheep.[18]
Later he told a Canaanite woman, who had appealed to him on behalf
of her demon-possessed daughter, that he 'was sent only' to Israel's
lost sheep.[19] This sounds disturbing, even shocking, until we
remember that it was just a temporary limitation, relating only to
Jesus' earthly ministry. He added that through his death, resurrection and the gift of the Spirit, salvation would be offered to all the
nations. And Jesus therefore later instructed his followers to take
the good news to these nations.

Even the Gospel of Matthew, the most Jewish of the four Gospels,
makes this global horizon clear. It begins with the genealogy of Jesus,
which is traced to Abraham, surely to indicate that the promise of
blessing to the nations is at last to be fulfilled.[20] Next, after the birth
of Jesus, Matthew describes the visit of those mysterious Magi, who
brought their treasures to 'the king of the Jews'. Matthew sees them
as forerunners of the Gentile multitudes who would later do homage
to Jesus.[21] Matthew also records Jesus' remarkable prediction that
'many will come from the east and the west, and will take their places
at the feast with Abraham, Isaac and Jacob in the kingdom of

heaven'.[22] And Matthew's Gospel ends with the fullest version of the so-called 'Great Commission'. The mission of the Twelve during Jesus' public ministry may have been restricted to 'the lost sheep of Israel', but the mission of the church has no such limitation. The followers of Jesus are to 'go and make disciples of all nations', welcoming them by baptism into the Christian community, and teaching them to obey all their Master's instructions.[23]

This commission to the nations has never been rescinded. It is still binding on the people of God. It was issued by the risen Christ who was able to claim that 'all authority in heaven and on earth' had been conferred on him. There is a clear link between the 'all authority' Jesus claimed and the 'all nations' he told us to disciple. The universal mission of the church springs from the universal authority of Jesus.

The Holy Spirit of the Acts is a missionary Spirit

Roland Allen, the influential missionary thinker, writes, 'The book of the "Acts" is strictly a missionary book . . . The conclusion is irresistible that the Spirit given was . . . in fact a missionary Spirit.'[24] This, he continues, is 'the great, fundamental, unmistakeable teaching of the book . . . It is in the revelation of the Holy Spirit as a missionary Spirit that the "Acts" stands alone in the New Testament.'[25]

Roland Allen was right. The Holy Spirit is the chief actor in the Acts. The book of Acts begins with the 120 disciples waiting. Before his death, Jesus had promised the coming of the Spirit and had described the Spirit's future ministry of convincing, teaching and witnessing. During the forty days between the resurrection and the ascension, Jesus told his disciples to wait for the Spirit who would give them 'power' for witness.[26]

So Pentecost was a missionary event. It was the fulfilment of God's promise through the prophet Joel to pour out his Spirit 'on all people',[27] irrespective of their race, sex, age or social standing. And the foreign languages which the disciples spoke (which seem clearly to have been what the 'tongues' were, at least on the Day of Pentecost) were a dramatic sign of the international nature of the Messiah's kingdom which the Holy Spirit had come to establish.

The rest of the Acts is a logical unfolding of that beginning. We watch enthralled as the missionary Spirit creates a missionary people and thrusts them out on their missionary task. They began to witness to their fellow Jews in and around Jerusalem, the Jewish headquarters. Then Philip took the bold initiative to witness to Samaritans, who were a halfway house between the Jews and the Gentiles.[28] Next came the conversion of the centurion Cornelius, one of those Gentile 'God-fearers' who accepted the monotheism and ethical standards of the Jews, but remained a Gentile, on the fringe of the synagogue without accepting full conversion. The Holy Spirit gave the clearest possible evidence that Cornelius was now a fully accredited member of the church.[29] Soon afterwards some unknown believers took the plunge and 'began to speak to Greeks also, telling them the good news about the Lord Jesus'.[30] The three missionary journeys of Paul the apostle to the Gentiles followed, in which he evangelized the provinces of Galatia, Asia, Macedonia and Achaia, the Holy Spirit both restraining and leading him.[31] The book ends with Paul in Rome, the capital of the world and the city of his dreams, not as a free man but as a prisoner. Yet still he was an indefatigable evangelist, preaching Jesus and the kingdom to all who visited him, 'with all boldness and without hindrance'.[32]

Throughout the Acts, Luke makes it plain that the impetus for mission came from the Holy Spirit. The book of Acts, writes Harry Boer, 'is governed by one dominant, overriding and all-controlling motif. This motif is the expansion of the faith through missionary witness in the power of the Spirit . . . Restlessly the Holy Spirit drives the church to witness, and continually churches rise out of the witness.'[33] Boer also points out that the momentum for this evangelism came from the Holy Spirit, not from the Great Commission, which in fact is not mentioned again after Acts 1. He writes, 'We must cease preaching the Great Commission as a command to be obeyed, but must present it *as a law that expresses the nature, and that governs the life, of the church* ... The outpouring of the Spirit is in and by reason of its (? his) very nature the effectuation of the Great Commission in the life of the church.'[34]

The church of the Letters is a missionary church

The members of the local church (whether in imagination or in reality) are often seen sitting in a circle facing each other. This picture is not entirely wrong, for we belong to each other and need each other's support. Indeed, we are often urged in the New Testament to love, encourage, comfort and exhort one another, and bear one another's burdens. And this 'one anotherness' of the Christian fellowship can be enjoyed and developed only as we face one another. Although legitimate, however, 'meeting in a circle' is also dangerous. For whenever we turn inwards towards one another, we have turned our backs on the world. To enjoy mutual fellowship we have also isolated ourselves from the world. That is fine as long as it is only temporary. We come apart from the world for worship and fellowship, in order to return to it strengthened to live as Christ's witnesses and servants.

The twenty-one Letters of the New Testament, even those addressed to individuals, are all intended in their different ways to build up the church so that it grows in both maturity and extent. True, the Letters address the domestic affairs of the church – its doctrine, worship, ministry, unity and holiness. But they also assume throughout that the church lives in the world and is responsible to reach out in compassion towards it.

Paul assumes that the churches will share in his own apostolic ministry through their support, their gifts and above all their prayers. He thanks God for the Philippians' 'partnership in the gospel'.[35] He asks the Thessalonians to pray that through him 'the message of the Lord may spread rapidly and be honoured'.[36] He asks the Colossians to pray that God will 'open a door for our message',[37] and the Ephesians that he may be given clarity and boldness in his preaching.[38]

The apostles also assume that the church will itself be involved in spreading the faith. Paul calls it 'the pillar and foundation of the truth',[39] which suggests that it must hold the truth high (like pillars thrusting up a building), and hold it firm (acting like a structure's foundation). Peter calls the church 'a chosen people, a royal priesthood, a holy nation, God's special possession', in order that its members may 'declare the praises' or 'proclaim the triumphs' (NEB) of the Saviour who has called them 'out of darkness into his wonderful light'.[40]

And each local church is to exhibit the missionary character of the whole church. The Philippians, who lived 'in a crooked and depraved generation', were told both to 'shine like stars in the sky' and to 'hold firmly to the word of life', displaying it as a merchant does his goods, or as a waiter the dishes at a feast.[41] The Thessalonians are described as having not only 'welcomed' the Lord's message, but as having made it ring out in the neighbouring regions.[42]

Individual church members are also to be involved in Christian witness. The apostles urge them to be conscious of the 'outsiders' who are watching them. 'Be wise in the way you act towards outsiders; make the most of every opportunity. Let your conversation be always full of grace, seasoned with salt, so that you may know how to answer everyone.'[43] It is a very practical instruction. We are to be wise in the way we relate to outsiders, to seize every chance to witness, to combine grace with salt (perhaps wholesomeness or even wit) in our conversation, and to be ready to answer whatever questions are put to us. This last point reminds us of Peter's direction: 'Always be prepared to give an answer to everyone who asks you to give the reason for the hope that you have.'[44]

So the church of the Letters is a missionary church, whether we are thinking of the universal church or the local church or individual church members. Mission is an essential part of the church's identity. In Bishop Lesslie Newbigin's forthright words, 'The commission to disciple all the nations stands at the centre of the church's mandate, and a church that forgets this, or marginalizes it, forfeits the right to the titles "catholic" and "apostolic".'[45]

The climax of the Revelation is a missionary climax

When John was permitted a peep through the 'door standing open in heaven',[46] he saw a great crowd of people standing before God's throne. They were wearing white robes (the symbol of righteousness) and holding palm branches (the symbol of victory), and they were joining in a mighty chorus of worship, attributing their salvation to God and to the Lamb. John also describes this great multitude as coming 'from every nation, tribe, people and language'.[47] The mission of the church will not be fruitless. On the contrary, it will result in a huge gathering in of people, a multiracial and multinational crowd. And their different languages and cultures will enrich their ceaseless celebration of the grace of God.

The redeemed multitude will also be countless. Only then will God's ancient promise to Abraham be completely fulfilled. To emphasize the limitless numbers of Abraham's descendants, both physical (the Jews) and spiritual (believers, whether Jews or Gentiles), God promised that they would be as numerous as the dust of the earth,[48] the stars in the sky[49] and the sand on the seashore.[50] Each metaphor symbolizes numberlessness. 'I will make your offspring like the dust of earth, so that *if anyone could count the dust*, then your offspring could be counted.'[51] 'Look up at the sky and count the stars – *if indeed you can count them*.'[52] Although we must be content to remain agnostic about how God will achieve this end, we can rejoice that the missionary labours of the church will come to such a glorious and God-honouring climax.

From this rapid overview of Scripture, we have seen that

- the God of the Old Testament is a missionary God, for he called one family in order to bless all the earth's families;
- the Christ of the Gospels is a missionary Christ, for he commissioned the church to go and make disciples of the nations;
- the Holy Spirit of the book of Acts is a missionary Spirit, for he drove the church out to witness;
- the church of the Letters is a missionary church, for it is a worldwide community with a worldwide task;
- the climax of the book of Revelation will be a missionary climax, for it involves a countless, international crowd.

So the religion of the Bible is a missionary religion. The evidence is overwhelming and irrefutable. Mission cannot be regarded as a regrettable deviation from religious toleration, or as the hobby of a few eccentric enthusiasts. On the contrary, it arises from the heart of God himself, and is communicated from his heart to ours. Mission is the global outreach of the global people of a global God.

We therefore need to repent if we have

- resisted the missionary dimension of the church's life;
- dismissed it as if it were dispensable;
- merely gestured towards it with a few perfunctory prayers and grudging coins;
- become preoccupied with our own narrow-minded, parochial concerns.

47

Do we profess to believe in God? He's a missionary God. Do we say we are committed to Christ? He's a missionary Christ. Do we claim to be filled with the Spirit? He's a missionary Spirit. Do we delight in belonging to the church? It's a missionary society. Do we hope to go to heaven when we die? It's a heaven filled with the fruits of the missionary enterprise. It is not possible to avoid these things.

If some of us need to repent, all of us need to take action. The authentic Christianity of the Bible is not a safe, smug, cosy, selfish, escapist little religion. On the contrary, it is deeply disturbing to our sheltered security. It is an explosive, centrifugal force, which pulls us out from our narrow self-centredness and flings us into God's world to witness and to serve. So we must find practical ways, individually and through our local church, of expressing this commitment.

In 1885, General William Booth, the founder of the Salvation Army, 'his eyes twinkling, challenged a mass rally of London Salvationists: "How wide is the girth of the world?" From the serried ranks came the full-throated response: "Twenty-five thousand miles." "Then," roared Booth, arms outspread, "we must grow till our arms get right round about it."'[53]

Reflection questions from Tim Chester

1 Which attitude towards Christian mission do you find among your unbelieving friends?
2 How would you respond to the accusation that mission is intolerant, arrogant or violent?
3 What is the difference between evangelism and proselytism? Can you think of examples of what Stott calls 'unworthy witness'?
4 What does it mean to call God a 'missionary God'? Describe the role of the Father, Son and Spirit in global mission.

5 Stott says, 'The authentic Christianity of the Bible is not a safe, smug, cosy, selfish, escapist little religion. On the contrary, it is deeply disturbing to our sheltered security. It is an explosive, centrifugal force, which pulls us out from our narrow self-centredness and flings us into God's world to witness and to serve.' Are there attitudes of which you need to repent?

6 In what practical ways, individually and in your church, could you express this commitment to global mission?

3

Holistic mission

'We Christians are the only people on this earth who have the integrated world view of matter and spirit that enables us to tackle sewer system development and the salvation of souls with equal gusto.'[1] So says Raymond Bakke. Carl Henry says evangelical Christians have a message doubly relevant to our day: 'For they know *the God of justice and of justification* . . . Whenever Christianity has been strong in the life of a nation, it has had an interest in both law and gospel, in the state as well as the church, in jurisprudence and in evangelism.'[2]

'Holistic mission' (from 'holism', the idea that the whole is greater than the sum of its parts) is an attempt, perhaps not an entirely satisfactory one, to capture the idea that authentic mission is a comprehensive activity that embraces both evangelism and social action, and refuses to let them be divorced.

But such 'both-and' statements do not define the *relationship* between evangelism and social responsibility. In recent decades there has been considerable disagreement about how these two responsibilities connect. It has been stated in different ways as the tension

- 'between God's action in and through the church and everything God is doing in the world apparently independently of the Christian community';[3]
- 'between the vertical interpretation of the gospel as essentially concerned with God's saving action in the life of individuals, and the horizontal interpretation of it as mainly concerned with human relationships in the world';[4]
- between God seeking the justification of sinners and God seeking justice in the nations;

- between redemption and providence;
- between the salvation of the soul and the improvement of society.

At times the difference between these viewpoints has become a sterile polarization, usually along the lines of the evangelical–liberal divide, each overreacting to the other's position. The former has tended to focus exclusively on evangelism to the neglect of social need, whether food for the hungry or freedom for the oppressed. The latter has gone to the opposite extreme and has tended to neglect evangelism, or tried to reinterpret it in socio-political terms as the humanization of communities or the liberation of the downtrodden. Thus, the evangelical stereotype has been to spiritualize the gospel, and deny its social implications, while the ecumenical stereotype has been to politicize it, and deny its offer of salvation to sinners. This polarization has been a disaster.

The relationship between evangelism and social responsibility

In the 1974 Lausanne Covenant, a broad range of evangelicals affirmed 'that evangelism and socio-political activity are both part of our Christian duty', adding that 'in the church's mission of sacrificial service evangelism is primary'.[5] The 1982 Consultation on the Relationship between Evangelism and Social Responsibility explained this primacy in two ways. First, evangelism has a certain logical priority: 'The very fact of Christian social responsibility presupposes socially responsible Christians, and it can only be by evangelism and discipling that they have become such.' Second,

> evangelism relates to people's eternal destiny, and in bringing them good news of salvation, Christians are doing what nobody else can do. Seldom if ever should we have to choose between . . . healing bodies and saving souls . . . Nevertheless,

51

if we must choose, then we have to say that the supreme and ultimate need of all humankind is the saving grace of Jesus Christ, and that therefore a person's eternal, spiritual salvation is of greater importance than his or her temporal and material well-being.[6]

In 1989 the Manila Manifesto made a similar statement: 'Evangelism is primary because our chief concern is with the gospel, that all people may have the opportunity to accept Jesus Christ as their Lord and Saviour.'[7]

To reaffirm the primacy of evangelism does not solve the problem, however. It leaves the relationships between evangelism and social responsibility still undefined.

It was to tease out these relationships that the Consultation on the Relationship between Evangelism and Social Responsibility was convened in 1982. Its final report identified three links between evangelism and social action. First, 'social activity is a *consequence* of evangelism'. For evangelism brings people to faith, faith works through love, and love issues in service.[8] Indeed, 'social responsibility is more than a consequence of evangelism; it is also one of its principal aims', since we are saved 'unto good works'.[9] Second, 'social activity can be a *bridge* to evangelism'. In spite of the danger of making 'rice Christians' (that is, those who profess conversion only because of the material benefits they are offered), it remains true that love in action 'can break down prejudice and suspicion, open closed doors, and gain a hearing for the gospel'. Third, 'social activity not only follows evangelism as its consequence and aim, and precedes it as its bridge, but also accompanies it as its *partner.* They are like the two blades of a pair of scissors or the two wings of a bird', as they were in the public ministry of Jesus. 'The partnership is, in reality, a marriage.'[10]

This partnership applies both to the individual Christian and to the local church. Of course, different Christians receive different specialist gifts and callings, qualifying them to concentrate on specialist ministries, just as the Twelve were called to a pastoral ministry and the Seven to a social ministry.[11] Of course, too, Christians may find themselves in emergency situations which demand specialized responses. We do not blame either the good Samaritan for tending the traveller's wounds and not enquiring into his spiritual state, or Philip for sharing the gospel with the Ethiopian and not enquiring into his social needs. Nevertheless, these are particular callings and situations. Generally speaking, all followers of Jesus Christ have a responsibility, according to the opportunities given to them, both to witness and to serve.

It is the same with each local church. The needs of its local community will be many and varied, and everyone cannot do everything. So, in a church of any size, its members should be encouraged to form 'study and action groups', according to their gifts, callings and interests, each taking up a particular evangelistic, pastoral or social need in the neighbourhood. The church must recognize these specialist groups, providing encouragement, advice, prayer and finance as necessary, and giving them opportunities to report on their progress. If it 'owns' the groups in this way, then the church will be able to reach out in compassion through them to the community and serve a number of different needs.

So far we have been thinking about the *relationships* between evangelism and social responsibility. The second problem we have concerns the *vocabulary* we should use to express the partnership between them. According to the report of the first National Evangelical Anglican Congress, 'evangelism and compassionate service belong together in the mission of God'.[12] I myself tried to elaborate this later by writing, '"Mission" describes . . . everything the church is sent into the world to do', namely 'Christian service in the world comprising both evangelism and social action'.[13]

Some evangelical leaders have criticized this definition of 'mission'. They believe it is potentially damaging because it will deflect missionaries from their priority tasks of evangelizing, discipling and church planting. They therefore want to retain the traditional understanding of 'mission' and 'missionary' as referring only to these evangelistic activities (although they often concede that all Christians have social and political responsibilities as well). Certainly, the last thing of which I want to be guilty is hindering the mission of the church! It is also true that 'mission' itself is not a biblical word, any more than 'Trinity' and 'sacrament' are. Yet it is a useful piece of shorthand for a biblical concept, namely all that Christ sends his people into the world to do. And this cannot be limited to proclamation evangelism, even if this has primacy in the church. The issue is not merely one of semantics (what does the word 'mission' mean?), but of substance (why are we sent into the world?). Even if I were to concede that the word 'mission' cannot bear the weight I have put on it, it would make no difference to the argument that we are sent into the world both to witness and to serve. And our mission is to be modelled on Christ's. Just as his love for us is like the Father's love for him,[14] so his sending of us into the world is like his Father's sending of him into the world.[15] If words and works went together in his ministry, they should do so in ours as well.

The main fear of my critics seems to be that missionaries will be sidetracked. The best way to avoid this, in my view, is not to deny that 'mission' is broader than evangelism, but rather to insist that each 'missionary' must be true to his or her particular calling. I have already suggested that in the local church, although individual members may have different foci, the church itself will be lopsided if it does not include a variety of ministries. In the same way, although some missionaries are called to primary evangelism, discipling, church planting and Bible translating, and others to specialist medical, educational or developmental ministries, the national church (and the mission agencies cooperating with it) would be lopsided if together they did not include such a variety of ministries.

Indeed, there is much to be said for multinational, multifunctional mission teams, composed of nationals and expatriates, evangelists and social workers, specialists in church planting and experts in development, pastors and teachers.

The biblical basis for this partnership

Evangelical Christians are nothing if not biblical Christians. Our desire is to live 'under' or 'according to' Scripture. Is there, then, good biblical warrant for holding evangelism and social action together? There is. It has been variously stated, but I will focus on three fundamental arguments.

First, there is *the character of God*.

The God of the biblical revelation, being both Creator and Redeemer, is a God who cares about the spiritual and material well-being of all the human beings he has made. Having created them in his own image, he longs that they will discover their true humanness in their relationships to him and each other. On the one hand, God yearns after his creatures in their lostness. He takes no pleasure in the death of the wicked, and is not willing that any should perish. So he begs them to listen to his Word, to return to him in penitence, and to receive his forgiveness. On the other hand, God cares for the poor and the hungry, the alien, the widow and the orphan. He denounces oppression and tyranny, and calls for justice. He tells his people to be the voice of the voiceless and the defender of the powerless. It is neither an accident nor a surprise, therefore, that God's two great commandments are that we love him with all our being and our neighbour as ourselves.

The outworking of these commandments is made clear in the law. For example, God's people were to 'fear', 'love' and 'serve' him. How? Partly by 'walking in his ways' and 'obeying his commands', because he is 'God of gods and Lord of lords', who on that account is to be worshipped; and partly by following his example as the one who 'defends the cause of the fatherless and the widow, and loves the foreigner . . . giving them food and clothing'.[16] Thus worship and obedience on the one hand, philanthropy and justice on the other, belong together as the double duty of the people of God.

Then came the prophets, who kept reminding the people of the law and urging them to obey it. 'He has showed you, O mortal, what is good. And what does the LORD require of you? To act justly and to love mercy and to walk humbly with your God.'[17] Again, justice and mercy to the neighbour and humility before God are united.

Alongside this prophetic witness to God's law went bold denunciations of those who flouted it. Elijah was an outstanding example. Living in a time of national apostasy, his ministry was encapsulated in his two major confrontations, first at Mount Carmel when he challenged the people to choose between Yahweh and Baal,[18] and then at Jezreel when he accused King Ahab of murdering Naboth and confiscating his property.[19] It is striking to find the same prophet acting as the champion of both religious loyalty and social justice.

Then 150 years later we find the two great exilic prophets, Jeremiah and Ezekiel, continuing the same tradition of protest. Why was disaster to fall upon Jerusalem? According to Jeremiah, because the people had 'forsaken' Yahweh in favour of 'foreign gods' and had filled Jerusalem with 'the blood of the innocent'.[20] According to Ezekiel, the city would bring down judgment upon itself 'by shedding blood in her midst and . . . by making idols'.[21] In both cases the acme of Israel's sin was the combination of 'idols' and 'blood' – idolatry being the worst sin against God, and murder the worst against the neighbour.

The law and the prophets thus reflect the character of God. What he is, his people must be also, sharing and reflecting his concerns. In particular, there is no dualism in the thinking of God:

We tend to set over against one another in an unhealthy way soul and body, the individual and society, redemption and creation, grace and nature, heaven and earth, justification and justice, faith and works. The Bible certainly distinguishes between these, but it also relates them to each other, and it instructs us to hold each pair in a dynamic and creative tension.[22]

The second ground for keeping evangelism and social concern together is *the ministry and teaching of Jesus*.

There can be no question that words and works went together in his public ministry. True, he was a preacher who announced the coming of the kingdom of God. But he also demonstrated its arrival by his works of compassion and power. 'He went about among the villages teaching',[23] and 'he went about doing good and healing'.[24] The similarity between these statements is the fact that 'he went about'; he had an itinerant ministry in which he criss-crossed the Palestinian countryside. The dissimilarity concerns what he 'went about' for. According to Mark it was 'teaching', according to Luke 'doing good and healing'. There was in his ministry an indissoluble bond between evangelism and compassionate service. He exhibited in action the love of God he was proclaiming. 'He was concerned,' Chuck Colson has written, 'not only with saving man from hell in the next world, but with delivering him from the hellishness of this one.'[25]

So his words explained his works, and his works dramatized his words. Hearing and seeing, voice and vision, were joined. Each supported the other. For words remain abstract until they are made concrete in deeds of love, while works remain ambiguous until they are interpreted by the proclamation of the gospel. Words without works lack credibility; works without words lack clarity. So Jesus' works made his words visible; his words made his works intelligible.

What Jesus exhibited in his life and ministry he also included in his teaching. Let me share a reflection on two of his best-known, best-loved parables, namely those of the prodigal son[26] (which highlights conversion) and the good Samaritan[27] (which highlights social action). If we hold them together, they enforce the connection between evangelism and social action.

In both parables there is a victim, a man who finds himself in a desperate plight. In the parable of the prodigal son he is the victim of his own sin; in the good Samaritan he is the victim of other people's sins, that is, he is sinned against. Moreover, in the first parable it is personal sin which is described; in the second it is social sin, namely the evil of public disorder. Both should arouse our compassion. We are concerned both for the sinning and for the sinned against.

Second, in both parables there is a rescue – from alienation in a distant land and from violent assault on the road. In the first parable the sinner repents, comes back and is forgiven (it is salvation by faith). In the second the victim can do nothing; he owes his rescue to the charity of the Samaritan (it is a rescue by good works).

Third, in both there is a display of love. In the prodigal son we see the love of God, as the father welcomes the boy home. In the good Samaritan we see the love of neighbour for neighbour, as the Samaritan binds up the victim's wounds. In both cases love triumphs over prejudice. The prodigal is forgiven *although* he does not deserve it; the Samaritan takes pity on the robbers' victim *although* he is an unknown Jew who has no claim on him.

Fourth, in both parables there is a sub-plot, which dramatizes the alternative to what is being commended. In the prodigal son, his elder brother refuses to rejoice in his brother's repentance and return. In the good Samaritan, the priest and Levite refuse to get involved in the battered man's plight. We might even say that those who resist the call to evangelism, and leave people alone in their sins, resemble the elder brother. Meanwhile, those who resist the call to social action, and leave people alone in their sufferings, resemble the priest and Levite who 'passed by on the other side'.

Thus each parable emphasizes a vital aspect of Christian discipleship – its beginning when, like the prodigal son, we come home for salvation, and its continuing when, like the good Samaritan, we go out in mission. Each of us resembles the prodigal; each of us *should* resemble the Samaritan. First, we face our own sins, and then we face the world's sufferings. First, we come in and receive mercy, and then we go out and show mercy. Mercy cannot be shown until it has been received; but once it has been received, it must be shown to others. Let us not divorce what Christ has married. We have all been prodigals; God wants us all to be Samaritans too.

In addition to the example and teaching of Jesus Christ, I would like to mention his emotions. When Jesus came face to face with the 'last enemy', death, the language of John 11 indicates that he both 'snorted' with anger against this evil and then 'wept' with compassion for its victims. The same two emotions should motivate us whenever we find ourselves confronting evil – whether the evil of human lostness or the social evils of our day.

In 1890, General William Booth published *In Darkest England and the Way Out*. Booth wrote with deep feeling about the miseries caused by poverty, unemployment, homelessness, hunger, exploited labour, drunkenness, disease, slums, white slavery and prostitution. 'The blood boils with impotent rage at the sight of these enormities,' he confessed, 'callously afflicted, and silently borne by these miserable victims.'[28] Of course he longed for their conversion, and maintained that he always put salvation first. But 'what is the use of preaching the gospel,' he asked, 'to people whose whole attention is concentrated upon a mad, desperate struggle to keep themselves alive?'[29] 'In providing for the relief of temporary misery,' he added, 'I reckon that I am only making it easy where it is now difficult, and possible where it is now all but impossible, for men and women to find their way to the cross of our Lord Jesus Christ.'[30] In pursuit of this policy, the second part of his book contains an amazing array of proposals – for a farm colony, an overseas colony, a travelling hospital, 'the prison gate brigade', rescue homes for prostitutes, 'preventive homes for unfallen girls in danger', an 'enquiry office for lost people', 'refuges for the children of the streets', 'industrial schools', 'model suburban villages', 'the poor man's bank', a legal aid scheme for the poor, and so on. As this remarkable combination of social and spiritual concerns became known, 'inevitably public fancy endowed the Army with a slogan which has stuck ever since: "soup, soap and salvation"!'[31]

The third biblical argument for the partnership of evangelism and social action concerns *the communication of the gospel*.

How is the gospel to be made known? To begin with, it must be verbalized. Since God himself chose to communicate in words, Christians should not despise words nor share in the current disenchantment with speech as a medium of communication. There is a precision in verbal communication, whether the words are spoken or written, which is absent from all other media. At the same time, the personal Word of God 'became flesh', as a result of which people 'have seen his glory'.[32] If God's Word became visible, our words must too. We cannot announce God's love with credibility unless we also exhibit it in action. So we cannot stand aloof from those to whom we speak the gospel, or ignore their situation. We have to enter into their social reality and share in their sufferings. At that point, says J. H. Bavinck, our actions 'become preaching'.[33]

This brings us back to the ministry of Jesus:

We are called today to a similar integration of words and deeds. In a spirit of humility we are to preach and teach, minister to the sick, feed the hungry, care for prisoners, help the disadvantaged and handicapped, and deliver the oppressed. While we acknowledge the diversity of spiritual gifts, callings and contexts, we also affirm that good news and good works are inseparable.[34]

Five objections considered

Although the biblical basis for the partnership between evangelism and social responsibility appears to be well laid, a number of objections to it are raised.

First, *shouldn't Christians steer clear of politics?* Christians should be engaged in philanthropy, but not political involvement.

If we define politics narrowly as referring to the policies and programmes for legislative change developed by political parties, then it is true that Christians should not get involved unless they are prepared to do their homework. Politics is for the politicians who have gained the necessary expertise. There are few things more embarrassing than the sight of Christians pontificating on political issues from positions of ignorance.

The broader definition of 'politics', however, refers to the life of the *polis*, the city, and to the art of living together in community. In this sense all of us are involved in politics, since Jesus calls us to live in the secular world.

Social welfare is not enough. Campaigning for legislative change is an essential expression of neighbour-love. For example, we have to go

- beyond healing individuals to building hospitals where different medical specialities are concentrated;
- beyond feeding the hungry to the establishment of a new international economic order in which hunger is abolished;
- beyond binding up people's wounds like the good Samaritan to the task of ridding the Jericho road of robbers;
- beyond the fair treatment of slaves to the abolition of the institution of slavery itself.

There may be no explicit biblical warrant for these things, and certainly Jesus never called for the emancipation of slaves. But are we not profoundly thankful that his followers did centuries later? Political action defined as love seeking justice for the oppressed is a legitimate extrapolation from the biblical emphasis on the practical priorities of love.

Second, *isn't this going back to the old 'social gospel'?* No, it is not. We must distinguish between the social gospel of theological liberalism, developed by Walter Rauschenbusch at the beginning of the twentieth century, and the social implications of the biblical gospel. The 'social gospel' attempted to identify the kingdom of God with socialized society, and then spoke of socio-political action in terms of 'building the kingdom of God on earth'. The vision was proud, self-confident and Utopian. The social implications of the biblical gospel are different, however. Once we have become new people in Christ, and are members of his new society, we must accept the responsibility he gives us to permeate the old society as its salt and light.

Third, *isn't this social concern the same as 'liberation theology'?* No, again it is not. Our main evangelical critique of liberation theology is that it attempts to equate the social, political and economic liberation of human beings with the 'salvation' that Christ came, died and rose to win. It has also tended to endorse Marxist theories (especially its social analysis) and to espouse violence. Having said that, the total liberation of human beings from everything that oppresses, demeans or dehumanizes them is surely pleasing to God their Creator. I wish evangelical Christians had got in first with a truly *biblical* theology of liberation. But to equate material 'liberation' with 'salvation' is to misunderstand and misrepresent Scripture.

Fourth, *isn't it impossible to expect social change unless people are converted?* Once more, no, it isn't. Of course we long for people to be converted. But Jesus Christ through his people has had an enormous influence for good on society as a whole. Think, for example, of the rising standards of health and hygiene, the wider availability of education, the growing respect for women and children, the concern for human rights and civil liberties, better conditions in factories, mines and prisons, and the abolition of slavery and the slave trade.

Legislation can secure social improvement, even though it does not convert people or make them good. Even fallen human beings retain sufficient traces of the divine image to prefer justice to injustice, freedom to oppression, and peace to violence. Martin Luther King was right when he said, 'Morality cannot be legislated, but behaviour can be regulated. Judicial decrees may not change the heart, but they can restrict the heartless . . . The law cannot make an employer love me, but it can keep him from refusing to hire me because of the colour of my skin.'[35]

Fifth, *won't commitment to social action distract us from evangelism?* Yes, it might, but no, it need not. Certainly we should beware of this possibility. We should be grateful for evangelical watchdogs who bark loud and long if they see any signs of a diminished commitment to evangelism. But if we live in the light of Jesus' death, resurrection and ascension, our incentives to evangelism will be continuously renewed at that perennial spring. In particular, his exaltation to the supreme place of honour will give us a desire that he be given the glory due to his name. Then social action, far from diverting us from evangelism, will make it more effective by making the gospel more visible and more credible.

Some examples of the partnership

'Social action in mission,' wrote the American missiologist Dr R. Pierce Beaver, 'can be traced from the time of the apostles.' Moreover, 'concern was never limited to relief'; it included what today we call 'development', enabling communities to become self-reliant, whether by introducing improved plants and livestock, eliminating diseases, digging deeper wells for pure and constant water, or establishing schools. In addition, missionaries (and in time national churches) stood for social justice. They were

> constantly the protectors of native peoples against exploitation and injustice by government and commercial companies . . . They played a very important part in the abolishing of forced labour in the Congo. They resisted black-birding in the South Pacific. They fought fiercely for human rights in combating opium, foot-binding, and exposure [to death] of girl babies in China. They waged war against widow-burning, infanticide and temple prostitution in India, and above all broke the social and economic slavery of the caste system for the low and outcaste peoples.[36]

There was, in fact, a certain inevitability about these concerns. It was impossible for the early missionaries to proclaim the message of God's love in Christ for the salvation of sinners and at the same time ignore people's social conditions. The gospel itself obliged them to oppose whatever was incompatible with it, whether slavery in Africa, untouchability in India, or the exploitation of tribal people or the degrading poverty of the masses in Latin America. Similarly, it is impossible to evangelize in the West and turn a blind eye to the plight of the unemployed and the homeless, or of alienated young people and single-parent families in decayed and deprived inner-city areas. Has the gospel nothing to say about these things? Is our God interested only in bringing people to heaven, and not in improving their circumstances on earth? No, to ignore the dehumanizing evils of society, while preaching the humanizing influence of salvation, is to be guilty of an inner contradiction that misrepresents God and distorts the gospel. Compassionate involvement in other people's felt needs is part and parcel of incarnational mission. It is demanded by the gospel of Christ.

Dr David Howard describes his friend Gregorio Landero as 'one of the most gifted evangelists I have ever known'. He goes on:

As he travelled around in evangelistic outreach to many parts of northern Colombia, he became heavily burdened because the people to whom he was ministering concerning their souls were suffering for lack of nutrition. He agonized about how he could preach a gospel of salvation when they were starving and suffering diseases which could be avoided with more adequate help. He began to study the possibilities of a more full-orbed outreach of the gospel. The result, over several years of hard work, was the development of United Action, a programme of total outreach for the needs of people. Gregorio is the leader of United Action and has given the vision and impetus to the entire development of the programme. Today, along with his evangelistic preaching, he and his colleagues are helping people to improve agricultural methods, developing family poultry projects that will put more protein into their diet, teaching home hygiene, carrying on dental work, literacy work and other things which will develop the family and community life of the people. There have also been efforts to help conserve the natural resources which are a part of the total creation.[37]

Festo Kivengere from Uganda had a similar holistic vision and commitment. He was first and foremost an evangelist. And when he became Bishop of the Diocese of Kigezi, he continued his extra-ordinarily effective worldwide evangelistic ministry, in which many were won to Christ. But he also concerned himself with development in his diocese, and especially with improved education, health and agriculture. His message centred on love and reconciliation through Christ, but he also pleaded for justice. Although not a political bishop in the sense that he took no part in the work of the legislative, judicial or executive functions of the state, he nevertheless played a major role in the overthrow of President Idi Amin. Several times he risked his life by confronting Amin in private and protesting against his reign of terror. 'Festo was so courageous,' his colleagues recalled. 'As the arrests continued, he kept going back to Amin to face him with the enormity of what he was doing.'[38]

Bishop Festo saw no inconsistency between these different aspects of his ministry. He spoke of 'the tragic divide between what, according to the Old Testament and the New Testament, are the two sides of the same coin – *the salvation of the lost souls of men . . .* and *the concern for their social needs*'.[39] Bishop Shannon Mallory said of him,

> Our dear Festo was a fiery prophet in the midst of that debate [i.e. about human rights violations being perpetrated at the time], calling passionately on the one hand for the spiritual renewal and reconciliation of the Church of Uganda, and at the same time boldly standing up (almost alone, it seemed) to speak out and condemn the political and military tyranny that was still going on in the country.[40]

Thus, evangelistic witness and political protest, far from being incompatible, were and are natural twins. Although few Christian people may be called to engage in them simultaneously, since different people are called to different ministries, nevertheless the church as a whole must engage in both, since both belong to its God-given mission in the world.

Reflection questions from Tim Chester

1 The report of the Grand Rapids Consultation (which Stott himself drafted) said social responsibility is (1) a consequence of, (2) bridge to and (3) partner of evangelism. Can you think of examples you have seen of each of these connections?

2 Why is evangelism primary? What might this look like in practice?

3 Which pressures do churches face to ignore social action and focus only on evangelism? How can we counter these pressures?

4 Which pressures do churches face to ignore evangelism and focus only on social action? How can we counter these pressures?

5 Why should Christians be involved in politics? What are the dangers of Christian political involvement?

6 What about you? Have you been neglecting evangelism, or social action, or both? Which two or three next steps could you take to make your discipleship more 'holistic'?

4

The Christology of mission

Nothing is more important for the recovery of the church's mission (where it has been lost), or its development (where it is weak), than a fresh, clear and comprehensive vision of Jesus Christ. When he is demeaned, and especially when he is denied, in the fullness of his unique person and work, the church lacks motivation and direction, our morale crumbles and our mission disintegrates. But when we see Jesus, it is enough. We have all the inspiration, incentive, authority and power we need.

In this chapter, then, we take a fresh look at our Lord and Saviour. We will rehearse the six major events in his saving career (his incarnation, cross, resurrection, exaltation, Spirit-gift and return), and we will note the inescapable (though often neglected) missionary dimension of each.

The incarnation of Christ

The model for mission

The incarnation was 'the most spectacular instance of cultural identification in the history of mankind'.[1] For the Son of God did not stay in the safe immunity of his heaven, remote from human sin and tragedy. He actually entered our world. He emptied himself of his glory and humbled himself to serve. He took our nature, lived our life, endured our temptations, experienced our sorrows, felt our hurts, bore our sins and died our death. He penetrated deeply into our humanness. He never stayed aloof from the people he might have been expected to avoid. He made friends with the drop-outs of society. He even touched untouchables. He could not have become more one with us than he did. It was the total identification of love.

I have sometimes compared Christ's mission to the earth with the Apollo mission to the moon. The analogy is shallow, no doubt, but it is instructive, for there are both similarities and dissimilarities between them. They are similar in that each is described as a 'mission', and consisted of a sensational, cross-cultural journey, in the case of Christ from heaven to earth, and of the astronauts from earth to moon. They are different, however, in the degree and depth of the identification involved. The Apollo astronauts never identified with the moon. If they had attempted to do so, they would have been dead in a moment. Instead, they took with them supplies from the earth – earth's oxygen, equipment, clothing and food. But when Jesus came from heaven to earth, he left heaven behind him and brought nothing but himself. His was no superficial touchdown. He became a human being like us, and so made himself vulnerable like us.

Yet when Christ identified with us, he did not surrender or in any way alter his own identity. For in becoming one of us, he nevertheless remained himself. He became human, but without ceasing to be God.

Now he sends us into the world, as the Father sent him into the world.[2] In other words, our mission is to be modelled on his. Indeed, all authentic mission is incarnational mission. It demands identification without loss of identity. It means entering other people's worlds, as he entered ours, though without compromising our Christian convictions, values or standards.

Paul was not a preacher to anonymous faces in the synagogue or in the open air. On the contrary, although he was free, he made himself everybody's slave. 'To the Jews I became like a Jew, to win the Jews . . . To those not having the law I became like one not having the law . . . so as to win those not having the law. To the weak I became weak, to win the weak. I have become all things to all people so that by all possible means I might save some.'[3] That is the principle of the incarnation. It is identification with people where they are.

In the history of missions there have been many dramatic examples of Christians trying to apply this principle. In 1732 Count Zinzendorf, the Moravian leader, sent two of his missionaries to the West Indian sugar plantations. They found that the only way to reach the African slaves was to join their chain gangs and share their huts.

In 1882 Major Frederick Tucker launched the Salvation Army in India. General Booth's last words to him were, 'Get into their skins, Tucker.' He did. Deeply concerned for the outcastes, he decided that he and his soldiers must live their life. So they donned saffron robes, adopted Indian names, walked barefoot, cleaned their teeth with charcoal and ate their curry sitting cross-legged on the floor.[4]

In 1950 a young Italian Roman Catholic priest, Mario Borelli, horrified by the loveless, homeless plight of the *scugnizzi*, Naples' street children, decided that the only way to reach them was to become one of them. He took on 'their dress, their speech, their habits'.[5] He may well have gone too far. And missionaries are not always wise to 'go native', 'principally because a foreigner's attempt to do this may not be seen as authentic but as play-acting'.[6] Nevertheless, one cannot but admire these daring attempts to follow the example of Christ's incarnation.

For most of us, however, the incarnational model will involve a more mundane struggle.

First, there is the need to enter into other people's *thought* world. I have always liked the title of Jim Sire's book, *The Universe Next Door*.[7] He sketches the meaning of deism, naturalism, nihilism, existentialism, Eastern pantheistic monism and so on. His point is that such people live in another universe of thought. It will therefore take a kind of incarnation to reach them. Similarly, John V. Taylor, the former Bishop of Winchester, says we will never be able to commend the gospel to modern sceptics 'so long as we remain inside our own cultural stockades'. 'Genuine outsiders,' he continues, 'can only be reached outside . . . If we do not naturally belong to the world of the particular "outsiders" we want to reach, some of us must take the trouble to cross over and learn to be at home in that alien territory.'[8]

We should, I believe, be praying and working for a whole new generation of Christian thinkers and apologists who will dedicate their God-given minds to Christ, entering sympathetically into their contemporaries' dilemmas and unmasking false ideologies. Then they will be able to present the gospel of Jesus Christ in such a way that he is seen to offer what other religious systems cannot, because he and he alone can fulfil our deepest human aspirations. In the West, where the Enlightenment has run out of steam, the time is now ripe, urges Bishop Lesslie Newbigin, for 'a genuinely missionary encounter with post-Enlightenment culture'.[9]

Second, we need to enter other people's *heart* world, the world of their angst and alienation, to weep with those who weep.[10] In every non-Christian (and many Christians too), even in the most extrovert, there are hidden depths of pain. We can reach them only if we are willing to enter into their suffering. This will also include entering into people's social reality, as we saw in the last chapter, for it is impossible to share the gospel with people in a social vacuum, isolating them from their actual context and ignoring their suffering.

The cross of Christ

The cost of mission

One of the most neglected aspects of biblical mission today is the indispensable place of suffering, even of death. Yet it is plain in Scripture. Let me give you three examples.

First, we see it in *Isaiah's suffering servant*. Before the servant can be a light to the nations and bring salvation to the ends of the earth,[11] he offers his back to those who beat him, his cheeks to those who pull out his beard, and his face to mockery and spitting.[12] Before he can 'sprinkle many nations',[13] he is 'despised and rejected by mankind, a man of suffering, and familiar with pain'.[14] More than that, he bears our sins and dies for us as a guilt offering.[15] Douglas Webster wrote,

> Mission sooner or later leads into passion. In biblical categories . . . the servant must suffer . . . it is that which makes mission effective . . . Every form of mission leads to some form of cross. The very shape of mission is cruciform. We can understand mission only in terms of the cross.[16]

Second, *the Lord Jesus himself* taught and exhibited this principle, and extended it to his followers. When some Greeks wanted to see him, he said, 'The hour has come for the Son of Man to be glorified [i.e. on the cross]. Very truly I tell you, unless a grain of wheat falls to the ground and dies, it remains only a single seed. But if it dies, it produces many seeds.'[17] In other words, only through his death would the gospel be extended to the Gentile world. So death is more than the way to life; it is the condition of fruitfulness. Unless it dies, the seed remains alone. But if it dies, it multiplies. It was so for the Messiah; it is the same for the messianic community. For 'whoever serves me must follow me', Jesus said.[18]

Third, *the apostle Paul* applied the same principle to himself. Consider these extraordinary texts:

> I ask you, therefore, not to be discouraged because of my sufferings for you, which are your glory.[19]

> Therefore I endure everything for the sake of the elect, that they too may obtain the salvation that is in Christ Jesus, with eternal glory.[20]

So then, death is at work in us, but life is at work in you.[21]

Paul dares to claim that through his sufferings others will enter into glory, that through his endurance others will be saved, and that through his death others will live. Is the apostle out of his mind? No! Does he really mean it? Yes! It is not, of course, that he attributes any atoning power to his own sufferings and death, as he does to the sufferings and death of Jesus Christ. Rather, people can receive salvation, life and glory only when the gospel is preached to them, and those who preach the gospel with faithfulness invariably suffer for it. Paul knew what he was talking about. The reason why he became a prisoner was that he had been faithful to the 'heavenly vision' that Gentiles would be received into the Christian community on precisely the same terms as Jews. It was this aspect of the gospel which aroused almost fanatical opposition to him. So the Gentiles owed their salvation to his willingness to suffer for his proclamation of this good news.

There have been many examples since Paul of suffering for the gospel. It is not an accident that the Greek word for 'witness' is *martys*, from which we get the English word 'martyr'. The pages of church history are full of stories of persecution. Sometimes it has been *physical*. In 1880, soon after the Salvation Army had been founded in Britain,

> publicans and brothel-keepers were launching a savage all-out counter-attack ... The Army learned the bleak truth of the Spanish proverb: 'He who would be a Christian must expect crucifixion' ... In one year – 1882 – 669 Salvation Army officers were knocked down or brutally assaulted. When Salvationists dedicated their children in the 1880s, they confessed their willingness that their children should be 'despised, hated, cursed, beaten, kicked, imprisoned or killed for Christ's sake'.[22]

At other times the suffering was more *mental* than physical. The Maréchale, for example, as the eldest daughter of General Booth was always known, wrote an article in 1883 for the *War Cry* from her prison cell in Neuchatel, Switzerland, in which she reflected on inward crucifixion:

> Jesus was crucified ... Ever since that day, men have tried to find an easier way, but the easier ways fail. If you would win thousands who are without God, you must be ready to be crucified: your plans, your ideas, your likes and your inclinations. Things have changed, you say, there is liberty now. Is there? Go and live Christ's life, speak as he spoke, teach what he taught, denounce sin wherever you find it, and see if the enemy will not turn on you with all the fury of hell ... Christ wasn't crucified in the drawing-room. His was no easy-chair business ... Do you shrink from being bated, misrepresented and spoken evil of? It is time you were crucified ...[23]

A third kind of suffering is *social*. Vincent Donovan, an American Roman Catholic priest who laboured for seventeen years among the Masai in Tanzania, once asked himself what the distinguishing mark of a missionary was. This is the answer he gave himself:

> A missionary is essentially a *social martyr*, cut off from his roots, his stock, his blood, his land, his background, his culture ... He must be stripped as naked as a human being can be, down to the very texture of his being ... [he must] divest himself of his very culture, so that he can be a naked instrument of the gospel to the cultures of the world.[24]

This call to suffering and death, as the condition for mission fruitfulness, sounds alien in our contemporary Western ears. The respectable middle-class captivity of the church is not exactly an arena for persecution. Where is the willingness to suffer for Christ today? In the evangelical tendency to triumphalism there seems little place for tribulation. And the false 'prosperity gospel', promising unlimited health and wealth, blinds people to the biblical warnings of adversity. Yet the fact remains that if we compromised less, we would certainly suffer more.

There are three main reasons for opposition; they belong to the spheres of doctrine, ethics and discipline:

1 As for doctrine, the gospel of Christ crucified remains folly to the intellectually proud and a stumbling-block to the self-righteous, so both groups find it humiliating.
2 As for ethics, Christ's call is to self-denial and self-control, so the self-indulgent find its challenge unacceptable.
3 As for discipline, both baptism and the Lord's Supper presuppose repentance and faith in those who wish to receive them, so to deny these gospel sacraments to anybody, even to those who openly admit that they neither repent nor believe, provokes outrage.

Thus, those who seek to be faithful in doctrine, ethics and discipline are sure to arouse persecution, in the church as well as in the world.

Are we ready, then, to bear the pain of being ridiculed, the loneliness of being ostracized, the hurt of being spoken against and slandered? Indeed, are we willing if necessary to die with Christ to popularity and promotion, to comfort and success, to our ingrained sense of personal and cultural superiority, to our selfish ambition to be rich, famous or powerful?

It is the seed that dies which multiplies.

A brother from Orissa, India, once told me that when he was eight years old his evangelist father had been martyred by hired assassins. At the time of his father's death, he added, there were only twelve churches in the region. When he spoke to me, there were 150.

The resurrection of Christ

The mandate for mission

It is of the greatest importance to remember that the resurrection preceded the Great Commission. It was the risen Lord who issued his commission to his followers to go and make disciples of all nations. He could not have issued it earlier, before he had been raised from death and invested with authority. 'All authority in heaven and on earth has been given to me,' he could now say. 'Therefore go and make disciples.'[25]

Johannes Blauw argued that the Old Testament perspective was one of 'universalism' (God promising that all the nations he had made would come and worship him),[26] but not of 'mission' (Israel going out to win the nations). The prophetic vision of the last days was of a 'pilgrimage of the nations' to Jerusalem. Mount Zion would be exalted as chief among the mountains, and 'all nations will stream to it'.[27] In the New Testament, however, this 'centripetal missionary consciousness' is replaced by a 'centrifugal missionary activity'.[28] That is, instead of the nations streaming to the church, the church now goes out to the nations. And what was the moment of change? 'The Great Turning-Point',[29] says Blauw, was the resurrection. It preceded the Great Commission to go, because all authority has now been given to Christ, in fulfilment of Daniel 7:13–14. 'With Easter a new age has begun, the enthronement of a new ruler of the world, and the proclamation of this new ruler among the nations. *Mission is the summons of the Lordship of Christ.*'[30]

'If the mission of the New Testament,' Blauw explains, 'seems at first glance centrifugal, it is to enable it to be centripetal. We go out into the world to gather it together; we cast the net to draw it in; we sow to reap.'[31] 'In Paul's own person the centripetal and centrifugal aspects of the preaching are brought together.'[32] That is, while going out to preach the gospel, he is gathering both Gentiles and Israel, and bringing them home.

The resurrection, however, is the key to both movements. It is the risen Lord who sends us out into the world, and it is the same risen Lord who gathers people in to his church. The universal mission of the church derives its legitimacy from the universal lordship of Christ. In this way, the resurrection supplies the mandate for mission.

The exaltation of Christ

The incentive for mission

Motivation is an important aspect of every human enterprise. We need to know not only *what* we should be doing, but *why* we should be doing it. When our motives are sound and strong, we can persist in any task. But when our motivation is faulty, we begin to flag. This is undoubtedly true of Christian mission. To seek to win people for Christ is hard work, widely unappreciated and unpopular, and, as we have just seen, it often provokes opposition. The church will need powerful incentives, therefore, if it is to persevere. The exaltation of Jesus Christ to the Father's right hand, that is, to the position of supreme honour, provides the strongest of all missionary incentives.

It is better in this context to refer to Christ's 'exaltation' than to his 'ascension'. For, although it is true that 'he ascended into heaven', yet to say that 'he was exalted' highlights the fact that God the Father vindicated, promoted, enthroned and invested his Son through the ascension. The apostolic statements about Jesus' exaltation are at pains to emphasize that he was raised above all possible rivals, indeed '*far above* all rule and authority, power and dominion, and every title that is invoked, not only in the present age but also in the one to come'.[33] This is 'the highest place' to which God has exalted Jesus[34] and the 'supremacy' which God wants him to enjoy.[35]

This throws light on the use of the word 'superiority', which is viewed with distaste by those who forsake the old exclusivism and inclusivism in favour of the new pluralism (see chapter 1). Certainly to adopt an 'air of superiority' towards the adherents of other faiths is a horrid form of discourtesy and arrogance. Certainly too, as Professor Hick points out, 'in the eighteenth and nineteenth centuries the conviction of the decisive superiority of Christianity' gave a powerful impetus to the imperial expansion of the West.[36] But it is not 'Christianity' as an empirical institution or system for which Christians should claim superiority. It is Christ, and only Christ. We should affirm without any sense of embarrassment or shame that he is 'superior' to all other religious leaders, precisely because he alone humbled himself, in love, to the cross and therefore God has raised him 'above' every other person, rank or title.

In the light of Christ's elevation or exaltation to the highest place, God desires 'every knee' to bow to him and 'every tongue' to confess his lordship.[37] The repeated 'every' is absolute; it allows no exceptions. If God has given this supreme honour to Jesus, and desires everybody else to honour him, then the people of God should share his desire. This is sometimes spoken of in Scripture in terms of 'zeal' or even 'jealousy'. The prophet Elijah, for example, deeply distressed by the apostasy of Israel, in particular their worship of the Canaanite Baals, said, 'I have been very zealous for the LORD, the God of hosts.'[38] The apostle Paul spoke of himself as 'jealous . . . with a godly jealousy' for the Corinthians, because he had betrothed them to Christ as their one husband, but was afraid that they might now be led astray from their 'sincere and pure devotion to Christ'.[39] Similarly, Henry Martyn, that brilliant and faithful Christian missionary in Muslim Iran towards the beginning of the nineteenth century, once said, 'I could not endure existence if Jesus were not glorified; it would be hell to me if he were to be always thus dishonoured.'[40]

This same sense of pain whenever Jesus Christ is dishonoured, and this same sense of jealousy that he should be given the honour due to him, should stir within us, in whatever particular culture we live. The primary motive for mission is neither obedience to the Great Commission, nor even love for those who are oppressed, lonely, lost and perishing, important as both those incentives are. Our primary motive is zeal or 'jealousy' for the glory of Christ. It was 'for his name's sake',[41] in order that it might receive the honour which it deserved, that the first missionaries went out. The same passionate longing should motivate us.

This, surely, is our answer to those who tell us that we should no longer evangelize or seek conversions. Professor Gregory Baum, for example, has said that 'after Auschwitz the Christian churches no longer wish to convert the Jews', for 'the churches have come to recognize Judaism as an authentic religion before God, with independent value and meaning, not as a stage on the way to Christianity'.[42] Similarly, a Greek bishop, on his resignation, wrote to his friends, 'As a bishop, a preacher of the gospel, I never tried to convert a Jew or Arab Moslem to Christianity; rather to convert them to be a better Jew, a better Moslem.'[43] Have these men, then, no jealousy for the honour of Jesus Christ? Do they not care when he is despised and rejected? Do they not long, as God does, that all human beings, whatever their culture or religion, will bow their knee to Jesus, and submit to him as their Lord?

It is this zeal for Christ which integrates the worship and witness of the church. How can we worship Christ and not mind that others do not? It is our worship of Christ that compels us to witness to Christ, in order that others may come and worship him too.

The Spirit-gift of Christ

The power for mission

John R. Mott, the leading figure behind the 1910 World Missionary Conference in Edinburgh, identified four requirements for world evangelization. He began with (1) an adequate plan, (2) an adequate home base and (3) an efficient church on the mission field. The fourth requirement he called 'the super-human factor'. He went on to say that, although missionaries, nationals and mission leaders may disagree about plans, means and methods, they

> are absolutely united in the conviction that the world's evangelization is a divine enterprise, that the Spirit of God is the great Missioner, and that only as he dominates the work and workers can we hope for success in the undertaking to carry the knowledge of Christ to all people. They believe that he gave the missionary impulse to the early church, and that today all true mission work must be inaugurated, directed and sustained by him.[44]

Already during his public ministry Jesus had drawn attention to the missionary purpose of the Holy Spirit. He had likened him to 'rivers of living water' irrigating the desert, and had promised that they would flow out from within every believer.[45] 'No one can . . . be indwelt by the Spirit of God,' comments William Temple, 'and keep that Spirit to himself. Where the Spirit is, he flows forth; if there is no flowing forth, he is not there.'[46] And so it proved to be in the early church from the Day of Pentecost onwards, as we saw in chapter 2.

There are, of course, differences between and within the churches regarding the Charismatic Movement, the so-called 'baptism of the Spirit', the diversity of spiritual gifts, and the place of 'signs and wonders' in evangelism. But all of us should be able to affirm that evangelism is impossible without the Holy Spirit, without God the Evangelist, as Professor David Wells calls him in a book of that title.[47] The Manila Manifesto says,

> The Scriptures declare that God himself is the chief evangelist. For the Spirit of God is the Spirit of truth, love, holiness and

power, and evangelism is impossible without him. It is he who anoints the messenger, confirms the Word, prepares the hearer, convicts the sinful, enlightens the blind, gives life to the dead, enables us to repent and believe, unites us to the body of Christ, assures us that we are God's children, leads us into Christlike character and service, and sends us out in our turn to be Christ's witnesses. In all this the Holy Spirit's main preoccupation is to glorify Jesus Christ by showing him to us and forming him in us.

All evangelism involves spiritual warfare with the principalities and powers of evil, in which only spiritual weapons can prevail, especially the Word and the Spirit, with prayer. We therefore call on all Christian people to be diligent in their prayers both for the renewal of the church and for the evangelization of the world.

Every true conversion involves a power encounter, in which the superior authority of Jesus Christ is demonstrated. There is no greater miracle than this, in which the believer is set free from the bondage of Satan and sin, fear and futility, darkness and death.

Although the miracles of Jesus were special, being signs of his messiahship and anticipations of his perfect kingdom when all nature will be subject to him, we have no liberty to place limits on the power of the living Creator today. We reject both the scepticism which denies miracles and the presumption which demands them, both the timidity which shrinks from the fullness of the Spirit and the triumphalism which shrinks from the weakness in which Christ's power is made perfect.

We repent of all self-confident attempts either to evangelize in our own strength or to dictate to the Holy Spirit. We determine in future not to 'grieve' or 'quench' the Spirit, but rather to seek to spread the good news 'with power, with the Holy Spirit and with deep conviction'.[48]

There is an urgent need for us to humble ourselves before the sovereign Holy Spirit today. Sociological knowledge and communications expertise are important. Indeed, they are gifts of God to be used in evangelism. But we have to be careful that they do not diminish our reliance on the power of the Holy Spirit. Only the Holy Spirit can take words spoken in human weakness and carry them home with power to the mind, conscience and will of the hearers.[49] Only he can open the eyes of the blind to see the truth as it is in Jesus, unstop the ears of the deaf to hear his voice, and loosen the tongues of the dumb to confess that he is Lord. The Holy Spirit is the chief witness; 'without *his* witness, *ours* is futile.'[50]

The return of Christ

The urgency of mission

The attitude of the Twelve immediately after the ascension was all wrong. They had been commissioned to go 'to the ends of *the earth*', but they were standing on the Mount of Olives 'looking into *the sky*'![51] They were then promised that the Jesus who had just disappeared would in due time reappear. For this event they must wait; no amount of sky-watching would hasten it. Meanwhile, once they had been clothed with the Spirit's power, they must get on with their task. Earth, not sky, was to be their preoccupation. Thus, the four stages of the divine programme were plain. First, Jesus returned to the Father (ascension). Second, the Spirit came (Pentecost). Third, the church goes out to make disciples (mission). Fourth, Jesus will return (Parousia). Between the first and the fourth events, the ascension and the return, the disappearance and the reappearance of Jesus, there was to be an unspecified period. The gap was to be filled with the worldwide witness of the church. So the implied message of the angels after the ascension was this: 'You have seen him go. You will see him come. But between that going and coming there must be another. The Spirit must come, and you must go – into the world for Christ.'[52]

This is how the return of Jesus is linked with the mission of the church. The return will bring to an end the period of mission that began with Pentecost. We have only a limited time in which to complete our God-given responsibility. We need, then, to recover the eager expectation of Christ's return which the first Christians had, together with the sense of urgency it gave them. Jesus had promised that the end would not come until the gospel of the kingdom had been preached to all nations.[53] But we have no freedom to presume that we have plenty of time, and so drag our feet or slacken our pace in mission. On the contrary, the church is 'on the move – hastening to the ends of the earth to beseech all men to be reconciled to God, and hastening to the end of time to meet its Lord who will gather all into one'.[54] The two ends will coincide.

Judgment forms another important link between the church's mission and the Lord's return. 'We must all appear before the judgment seat of Christ,' Paul wrote, 'so that each of us may receive what is due to us.'[55] This is evidently not the universal judgment relating to our eternal destinies, but a particular judgment of God's people relating to our Christian life and ministry. It concerns the promise of recognition and recompense of some kind, or their opposite. The next verse reads, 'Since, then, we know what it is to fear the Lord, we try to persuade others.'[56] That is, the reason why we seek to persuade people of the truth of the gospel is that we stand in awe of the Lord Jesus and his tribunal, before which we will one day have to give an account. I am reminded of those solemn passages in the prophecy of Ezekiel,[57] in which God appoints him 'a watchman for the house of Israel' and makes him responsible to warn them of the coming judgment. If he fails to give the wicked adequate warning, and does not speak out to dissuade them from their evil ways, God says, 'I will hold you accountable for their blood.'[58]

In a similar way the apostle grounded his charge to Timothy to 'preach the word' with urgency not only on 'the presence of God and of Christ Jesus', but also 'in view of his appearing and his kingdom', who 'will judge the living and the dead'.[59] To live, work and witness in conscious anticipation of Christ's return and judgment is a healthy stimulus to faithfulness. Scripture calls us to remember that from God's perspective, the time is short, the need is great, and the task is urgent.

Summary

Let me sum up what Christ's saving career says to us about mission:

- the *model* for mission is his incarnation (identification without loss of identity);
- the *cost* of mission is his cross (the seed which dies multiplies);
- the *mandate* of mission is his resurrection (all authority is now his);
- the *motivation* of mission is his exaltation (the honour of his name);
- the *power* of mission is his gift of the Spirit (who is the paramount witness);
- the *urgency* of mission is his return (we will have to give him an account when he comes).

The church needs to keep returning for its inspiration and direction to this Christological basis of mission. The challenge before us is to see Jesus Christ as adequate for our task. We must repent of our pessimism (especially in the West), our low expectations, our cynical unbelief that although the church may grow elsewhere, it cannot grow among us. Rubbish! If only we could gain a fresh and compelling vision of Jesus Christ, incarnate and crucified, risen and reigning, bestowing the Spirit and coming again! Then we would have the clarity of purpose and strength of motive, the courage, the authority, the power and the passion for world evangelization in our time.

In an early anniversary sermon for the Church Missionary Society, John Venn, the Rector of Clapham, described a missionary in the following terms. His eloquent portrait is equally applicable to every kind of Christian witness:

> With the world under his feet, with heaven in his eye, with the gospel in his hand and Christ in his heart, he pleads as an ambassador for God, knowing nothing but Jesus Christ, enjoying nothing but the conversion of sinners, hoping for nothing but the promotion of the kingdom of Christ, and glorying in nothing but in the cross of Christ Jesus, by which he is crucified to the world, and the world to him.[60]

Reflection questions from Tim Chester

1 Think of the people among whom you live and work. Inspired by the incarnation of Jesus, what could you do to enter their *thought*-world and their *heart*-world?

2 Stott says, 'If we compromised less, we would assuredly suffer more.' In which ways have you suffered for the sake of mission? In which ways are you tempted to compromise to avoid suffering?

3 Look at 1 Peter 3:15. How does the lordship of the risen Christ shape mission? Peter calls us to explain the lordship of Christ with gentleness and respect. What happens when we affirm Christ's lordship without gentleness? What happens when we are gentle without affirming Christ's lordship?

4 Stott says, 'Zeal for Christ integrates the worship and witness of the church.' How can we ensure the worship of the church motivates us to be involved in mission?

5 What does it mean for you to be dependent on the Holy Spirit as you are involved in mission? How does it change your behaviour or attitudes?

6 Stott says we need to recover 'the sense of urgency' that Christ's return should give us, and 'we must repent of our pessimism and our low expectations'. How has this chapter challenged your attitudes? Of what do you need to repent?

Conclusion
The now and the not yet

I began in the Introduction with the tension between the 'then' (past) and the 'now' (present); I end with another tension, between the 'now' (present) and the 'not yet' (future). These two tensions belong together. For it is in and through Jesus Christ that the past, the present and the future are brought into a creative relationship. Christians live in the present, but do so in thankfulness for the past and in anticipation of the future.

As I conclude this book, I'm going to focus on balanced biblical Christianity. Balance is a rare commodity these days in almost every sphere, not least among us who seek to follow Christ.

One of the things about the devil is that he is a fanatic, and the enemy of all common sense, moderation and balance. One of his favourite pastimes is to tip Christians off balance. If he cannot get us to *deny* Christ, he will get us to *distort* Christ instead. As a result, lopsided Christianity is widespread, in which we overemphasize one aspect of a truth, while underemphasizing another.

A balanced grasp of the now–not-yet tension would be very beneficial for Christian unity, and especially to a greater harmony among evangelical believers. We may agree on the doctrinal and ethical fundamentals of the faith. Yet we seem to be constitutionally prone to quarrelling and dividing, or simply to going our own way and building our own empires.

Kingdom come and coming

Fundamental to New Testament Christianity is the perspective that we are living 'in between times' – between the first and the second comings of Christ, between kingdom come and kingdom coming.

The theological basis for this tension is to be found in Jesus' own teaching about the kingdom of God. Everyone accepts both that the kingdom featured prominently in his teaching and that he announced its coming. Where scholars have disagreed, however, is over the time of its arrival. Has the kingdom already come, because Jesus brought it with him? Or is its coming still in the future, so that we await it expectantly? Or does the truth lie between these positions?

Albert Schweitzer is an example of a scholar who thought that, according to Jesus, the kingdom lay entirely in the future. As an apocalyptic prophet, Jesus taught (mistakenly) that God was about to intervene supernaturally and establish his kingdom. The radical demands he made on his disciples were an 'interim ethic' in the light of the imminent arrival of the kingdom. Schweitzer's position is known as 'thoroughgoing' or 'consistent' eschatology.

At the opposite extreme was C. H. Dodd, with his belief that the coming of the kingdom is wholly in the past (known as 'realized eschatology'). He laid a heavy emphasis on two verses whose verbs are in the perfect tense, namely 'The kingdom of God has arrived'[1] and 'The kingdom of God has come upon you.'[2] Dodd concluded that there is no future coming of the kingdom, and that passages which speak of one were not part of Jesus' own teaching.

In place of these extreme polarities, most scholars have taken a middle position – that Jesus spoke of the kingdom as both a present reality and a future expectation.

Jesus clearly taught that the time of fulfilment had arrived;[3] that 'the strong man' was now bound and disarmed, enabling the plundering of his goods, as was evident from his exorcisms;[4] that the kingdom was already either 'within' or 'among' people;[5] and that it could now be 'entered' or 'received'.[6]

Yet the kingdom was a future expectation as well. It would not be perfected until the last day. So he looked forward to the end, and taught his disciples to do so also. They were to pray 'your kingdom come'[7] and to 'seek' it first,[8] giving priority to its expansion. At times he also referred to the final state of his followers in terms of 'entering' the kingdom[9] or 'receiving' it.[10]

One way in which the Bible expresses the tension between the 'now' and the 'not yet' is in the terminology of the two 'ages'. From the perspective of the Old Testament, history is divided between 'this present age' and 'the last days', namely the kingdom of righteousness to be introduced by the Messiah.[11] This simple structure of two consecutive ages was decisively changed, however, by the coming of Jesus. For he brought in the new age, and died for us in order to deliver us 'from the present evil age'.[12] As a result, the Father has already 'rescued us from the dominion of darkness and brought us into the kingdom of the Son he loves'.[13] We have even been raised from death and seated with Christ in the heavenly realm.[14]

At the same time, the old age persists. So the two ages overlap. 'The darkness is passing and the true light is already shining.' One day the old age will be terminated (which will be 'the end of the age'),[15] and the new age, which was introduced with Christ's first coming, will be brought about at his second. Meanwhile, the two ages continue, and we are caught in the tension between them. We are summoned not to 'conform to the pattern of this world', but rather to 'be transformed' according to God's will and to live consistently as children of the light.[16]

Nevertheless, the tension remains: we have already *been* saved, yet also we *shall* be saved one day.[17] And we are already God's adopted children, yet we also are waiting for our adoption.[18] Already we have 'crossed over from death to life', yet eternal life is also a future gift.[19] Already Christ is reigning, although his enemies have not yet become his footstool.[20]

Caught between the present and the future, the characteristic stance of Christians is variously described as hoping,[21] waiting,[22] longing,[23] and groaning,[24] as we wait both 'eagerly'[25] and also 'patiently'.[26]

The essence of the interim period between the 'now' and the 'not yet' is the presence of the Holy Spirit in the people of God. On the one hand, the gift of the Spirit is the distinctive blessing of the kingdom of God and the principal sign that the new age has dawned.[27] On the other, because his indwelling is only the beginning of our kingdom inheritance, it is also the guarantee that the rest will one day be ours. The New Testament uses three metaphors to illustrate this. The Holy Spirit is the 'firstfruits', pledging that the full harvest will follow,[28] the 'deposit' or first instalment, pledging that the full payment will be made,[29] and the foretaste, pledging that the full feast will one day be enjoyed.[30]

Here are some examples of the tension between the 'now' and the 'not yet'.

Revelation, holiness and healing

The first example is in *the intellectual sphere*, or the question of *revelation*.

We affirm with joyful confidence that God has revealed himself to human beings, not only in the created universe, in our reason and our conscience, but supremely in his Son Jesus Christ, and in the Bible's witness to him. We dare to say that we know God, because he has himself taken the initiative to draw aside the curtain which would otherwise hide him from us. We rejoice greatly that his Word throws light on our path.[31]

But we do not yet know God as he knows us. Our knowledge is partial because his revelation has been partial. He has revealed everything that he intends to reveal, and which he considers to be for our good, but not everything that there is to reveal. There are many mysteries left, and so 'we live by faith, not by sight'.[32]

We should take our stand alongside those biblical authors who, although they knew themselves to be agents of divine revelation, nevertheless confessed humbly that their knowledge remained limited. Even Moses, 'whom the LORD knew face to face', acknowledged, 'O Sovereign LORD, you have only [RSV] begun to show to your servant your greatness and your strong hand.'[33] Then think of the apostle Paul, who likened his knowledge both to the immature thoughts of a child and to the distorted reflections of a mirror.[34]

So then, although it is right to glory in the givenness and finality of God's revelation, it is also right to confess our ignorance of many things. We know and we don't know. 'The secret things belong to the LORD our God, but the things revealed belong to us and to our children for ever, that we may follow all the words of this law.'[35] It is very important to maintain this distinction. Speaking personally, I would like to see more boldness in our proclaiming what has been revealed, and more reticence about what has been kept secret. Agreement in plainly revealed truth is necessary for unity, even while we give each other freedom in secondary matters. And the way to recognize these is when Christians who are equally anxious to be submissive to Scripture nevertheless reach different conclusions about them. I am thinking, for example, about controversies over baptism, church government, liturgy and ceremonies, claims about spiritual gifts, and the fulfilment of prophecy.

The second tension is in *the moral sphere*, or the question of *holiness*.

God has already put his Holy Spirit within us, in order to make us holy.[36] The Holy Spirit is actively at work within us, subduing our fallen, selfish human nature and causing his fruit to ripen in our character.[37] Already, we can affirm, he is transforming us into the image of Christ.[38]

But our fallen nature has not been eradicated, for 'the flesh desires what is contrary to the Spirit',[39] so that 'if we claim to be without sin, we deceive ourselves'.[40] We have not yet become completely conformed to God's perfect will, for we do not yet love God with all our being, or our neighbour as ourselves. As Paul put it, we have 'not . . . already become perfect' (GNT), but we 'press on towards the goal', confident that 'he who began a good work in [us] will carry it on to completion until the day of Christ Jesus'.[41]

So then, we are caught in a painful tension between the 'now' and the 'not yet', between dismay over our continuing failures and the promise of ultimate freedom. On the one hand, we must take God's command, 'Be holy because I . . . am holy',[42] and Jesus' instruction, 'Go, and do not sin again',[43] with the utmost seriousness. On the other hand, we have to acknowledge the reality of indwelling sin alongside the reality of the indwelling Spirit.[44] The sinless perfection we long for continues to elude us.

The third tension between the 'already' and the 'not yet' is to be found in *the physical sphere* or the question of *healing*.

We affirm that the long-promised kingdom of God broke into history with Jesus Christ, who was not content merely to *proclaim* the kingdom, but went on to *demonstrate* its arrival by the extraordinary things he did. His power was especially evident in the human body as he healed the sick, expelled demons and raised the dead.

He also gave authority to both the Twelve and the Seventy to extend his mission in Israel, and to perform miracles. How much wider he intended his authority to go is a matter of dispute. Generally speaking, miracles were 'the signs of a true apostle'.[45] Nevertheless, it would be foolish to attempt to limit or domesticate God. We must allow him his freedom and his sovereignty, and be entirely open to the possibility of physical miracles today.

But God's kingdom has not yet come in its fullness. For 'the kingdom of the world' has not yet 'become the kingdom of our Lord and of his Christ' when 'he will reign for ever and ever'.[46] In particular, our bodies have not yet been redeemed, and nature has not yet been entirely brought under Christ's rule.

So we have to recognize the 'already'–'not-yet' tension in this sphere too. To be sure, we have 'tasted . . . the powers of the coming age',[47] but so far it has been only a taste. Part of our Christian experience is that the resurrection life of Jesus is 'revealed in our mortal body'.[48] At the same time, our bodies remain frail and mortal. To claim perfect health now would be to anticipate our resurrection. The bodily resurrection of Jesus was the pledge, and indeed the beginning, of God's new creation. But God has not yet uttered the decisive word, 'I am making everything new!'[49] Those who dismiss the very possibility of miracles today forget the 'already' of the kingdom, while those who expect them as what has been called 'the normal Christian life' forget that the kingdom is 'not yet'.

Church and society

Fourth, the same tension is experienced in *the ecclesiastical sphere*, or the question of *church discipline.*

Jesus the Messiah is gathering round him a people of his own, a community characterized by the truth, love and holiness to which he has called it. But Christ has not yet presented his bride to himself 'as a radiant church, without stain or wrinkle or any other blemish, but holy and blameless'.[50] On the contrary, her present life and witness are marred by error, discord and sin.

So then, whenever we think about the church, we need to hold together the ideal and the reality. The church is both committed to truth and prone to error, both united and divided, both pure and impure. Not that we are to accept its failures. We are to cherish the vision of both the doctrinal and ethical purity and the visible unity of the church. We are called to 'fight the good fight of the faith',[51] and to 'make every effort to keep the unity of the Spirit through the bond of peace'.[52] And in pursuit of these things there is a place for discipline in cases of serious heresy or sin.

And yet error and evil are not going to be eradicated completely from the church in this world. They will continue to coexist with truth and goodness. 'Let both grow together until the harvest,' Jesus said in the parable of the wheat and the weeds.[53] Neither the Bible nor church history justifies the use of severe disciplinary measures in an attempt to secure a perfectly pure church in this world.

The fifth area of tension between the 'now' and the 'then', the 'already' and the 'not yet', is *the social sphere*, or the question of *progress*.

We affirm that God is at work in human society. This is partly in his 'common grace', as he gives the world the blessings of family and government, by which evil is restrained and relationships are ordered. And it is also through the members of his redeemed community, who penetrate society like salt and light, making a difference by hindering decay and dispelling darkness.

But God has not yet created the promised 'new heaven and . . . new earth, the home of righteousness'.[54] There are still 'wars and rumours of wars'.[55] Swords have not yet been beaten into ploughshares and spears into pruning hooks.[56] The nations have not yet renounced war as a method of settling their disputes. Selfishness, cruelty and fear continue.

So then, although it is right to campaign for social justice and to expect to improve society further, we know that we shall never perfect it. Although we know the transforming power of the gospel and the wholesome effects of Christian salt and light, we also know that evil is ingrained in human nature and human society. Only Christ at his second coming will eradicate evil and enthrone righteousness for ever.

Here, then, are five areas (intellectual, moral, physical, ecclesiastical and social) in which it is vital to preserve the tension between the 'already' and the 'not yet'.

Three types of Christian

There are three distinct types of Christian, according to the extent to which they manage to maintain this biblical balance.

First, there are *the 'already' Christians* who emphasize what God has already given us in Christ. But they give the impression that, in consequence, there are now no mysteries left, no sins that cannot be overcome, no diseases that cannot be healed, and no evils that cannot be eradicated. In short, they seem to believe that perfection is attainable now.

Their motives are blameless. They want to glorify Christ – so they refuse to set limits to what he is able to do. But their optimism can easily degenerate into presumption and end up in disillusion. They forget the 'not yet' of the New Testament, and that perfection awaits the second coming of Christ.

Second, there are *the 'not-yet' Christians* who emphasize the incompleteness for the time being of the work of Christ and look forward to the time when he will complete what he has begun. But they seem to be preoccupied with our human ignorance and failure, the pervasive reign of disease and death, and the impossibility of securing either a pure church or a perfect society.

Their motive is excellent too. If the 'already' Christians want to glorify Christ, the 'not-yet' Christians want to humble sinners. They are determined to be true to the Bible in their emphasis on our human depravity. But their pessimism can easily degenerate into complacency; it can also lead to acceptance of the status quo and to apathy in the face of evil. They forget the 'already' of what Christ has done by his death, resurrection and gift of the Spirit – and of what he can do in our lives, and in church and society, as a result.

Third, there are *the 'already–not-yet' Christians*. They want to give equal weight to the two comings of Jesus. On the one hand, they have great confidence in the 'already', in what God has said and done through Christ. On the other hand, they exhibit a genuine humility before the 'not yet', humility to confess that the world will remain fallen and half-saved until Christ perfects at his second coming what he began at his first.

It is this combination of the 'already' and the 'not yet' which characterizes authentic biblical evangelicalism, and which exemplifies the balance that is so urgently needed today.

Our position as 'contemporary Christians' rests securely on the person of Jesus, whose death and resurrection belong to the 'already' of the past, and whose glorious second coming to the 'not yet' of the future. As we acclaim in faith and triumph:

Christ has died!
Christ is risen!
Christ will come again!

Notes

Preface
1 Revelation 1:8.
2 Hebrews 13:8.

**Series introduction: the Contemporary Christian –
the then and the now**
1 Psalm 119:105; cf. 2 Peter 1:19.
2 Dietrich Bonhoeffer, *Letters and Papers from Prison*, enlarged edn
   (SCM Press, 1971), p. 279.
3 Matthew 11:19.
4 See Jaroslav Pelikan, *Jesus Through the Centuries* (Yale University
   Press, 1985), pp. 182–193.
5 2 Corinthians 11:4.
6 2 Timothy 1:15; cf. 4:11, 16.
7 Acts 26:25.
8 Ezekiel 2:6–7.

The World: introduction
1 Cf. Matthew 5:16.

I The uniqueness of Jesus Christ
1 The story is told by Douglas Webster in *Not Ashamed* (Hodder &
   Stoughton, 1970), p. 66.
2 W. A. Visser 't Hooft, *No Other Name* (SCM Press, 1963), p. 11.
3 Ibid., p. 95.
4 These categories were first employed by Alan Race in *Christians
   and Religious Pluralism* (Orbis, 1982), were popularized by the
   Church of England General Synod's Board for Mission and Unity

in their report *Towards a Theology for Inter-Faith Dialogue* (Anglican Consultative Council, 1984; 2nd edn, 1986) and were further developed by Paul F. Knitter in *No Other Name?* (SCM Press, 1985), while the implications of 'pluralism' were explored in John Hick and Paul F. Knitter (eds.), *The Myth of Christian Uniqueness* (SCM Press, 1987). A judicious critique by Dr Christopher Wright of *Towards a Theology for Inter-Faith Dialogue* appeared in *Anvil* (vol. I, no. 3, 1984), and this material has now been incorporated in his booklet, *What's So Unique about Jesus?* (MARC, 1990). Then, in 1991 (too late to be considered in this book), there appeared a vigorous riposte to *The Myth of Christian Uniqueness* entitled *Christian Uniqueness Reconsidered: The Myth of a Pluralist Theology of Religions*, ed. Gavin D'Costa (Fowler Wright). It is another symposium, and includes contributions by such leading contemporary theologians as Jürgen Moltmann, Lesslie Newbigin, Wolfhart Pannenberg, Rowan Williams and M. M. Thomas.

5 *Gaudium et Spes*, para. 22.

6 This is one possible position described by Raimundo Panikkar in his contribution to *The Myth of Christian Uniqueness*, p. 91.

7 Stanley J. Samartha in *The Myth of Christian Uniqueness*, pp. 79–80.

8 Matthew 10:34.

9 Paul F. Knitter, *No Other Name?* (SCM Press, 1985), p. 2.

10 *The Myth of Christian Uniqueness*, p. 17.

11 Rosemary Radford Ruether in *The Myth of Christian Uniqueness*, p. 139.

12 Ibid., p. 76.

13 Tom F. Driver in *The Myth of Christian Uniqueness*, p. 207.

14 *The Myth of Christian Uniqueness*, pp. 39–40.

15 Ibid., p. viii.

16 Ibid., p. 8.

17 Ibid., pp. 12–13.

18 Ibid., p. 211.

19 Ibid., pp. 56–57.

20 Ibid., p. 59.

21 Ibid., p. 216.

22 Ibid., Part III.

23 Ibid., p. 180.

24 Ibid., pp. 23–30.

25 Ibid., p. 141.

26 The full text of his sermon appears in the *International Review of Mission*, July 1988, pp. 325–331.

27 John Mbiti, *African Religions and Philosophy* (Heinemann, 1969), p. 277.

28 Stanley Jones, *The Christ of the Indian Road* (1925; Hodder & Stoughton, 1926), p. 64.

29 Stephen C. Neill, *Crises of Belief* (Hodder & Stoughton, 1984), published in the United States as *Christian Faith and Other Faiths* (IVP USA, 1984), p. 23.

30 Ibid., p. 286.

31 See P. Carnegie Simpson, *The Fact of Christ* (1930; James Clarke, 1952), pp. 19–22.

32 2 Peter 3:18.

33 E.g. Acts 2:36; Romans 10:9; cf. Matthew 28:18.

34 Deuteronomy 6:4.

35 Chapter on Mary, in *The Koran*, translated by N. J. Dawood (Penguin, 1968), p. 34.

36 John Hick (ed.), *The Myth of God Incarnate* (SCM Press, 1977), p. 169.

37 Translated by Juan Mascaro, *Bhagavad Gita* (Penguin, 1962), pp. 61–62.

38 Quoted by W. A. Visser 't Hooft, *No Other Name* (SCM Press, 1963), pp. 36–37.

39 Colossians 2:9.

40 Luke 19:10.

41 Luke 15:1–7.

42 John 10:11, 15.

43 From an article in the *Church of England Newspaper* on 28 May 1976.

44 Emil Brunner, *The Mediator* (1927; ET Westminster, 1947), pp. 291–299.

45 C. G. Montefiore, *The Synoptic Gospels* (Macmillan, 2nd edn, 1927), vol. I, pp. cxviii, 55; vol. II, pp. 520–521.

46 S. C. Neill, *Crises of Belief*, p. 87.

47 T. Kagawa, *Christ and Japan* (SCM Press, 1934), pp. 108, 113.

48 Psalms 19:14; 23:1; 27:1; 62:2; 63:1.

49 Philippians 3:8.

50 1 Peter 1:8.

51 E.g. John 14:16–18; Romans 8:9–10.

52 Ephesians 3:16–17.

53 Ephesians 2:18.

54 John 14:16–23.

55 Stephen C. Neill, *Christian Faith Today* (Penguin, 1955), pp. 17–18.

56 Donald Coggan, *Paul: Portrait of a Revolutionary* (Hodder & Stoughton, 1984), p. 75.

57 Cf. Matthew 18:20.

58 Matthew 28:20.

59 P. F. Knitter, *No Other Name?*, p. 185.

60 *The Myth of Christian Uniqueness*, p. 196.

61 Matthew 11:25–27.

62 John 14:6.

63 Acts 4:10–12.

64 1 Corinthians 8:6.

65 Hebrews 10:12–14.

66 1 Timothy 2:5.

67 W. A. Visser 't Hooft, *No Other Name*, p. 102.

68 Matthew 28:18–29.

69 Acts 17:27–28.

70 John 1:1–5.

71 John 1:9.

72 Acts 11:14, 18; 15:9.

73 Revelation 7:9.

74 Genesis 22:17.

75 Romans 5:15–21.

76 Romans 10:14.

77 Romans 10:17.

2 Our God is a missionary God

1 From a letter to Lord Samuel, dated 26 November 1942, published in F. S. Temple (ed.), *Some Lambeth Letters* (OUP, 1963), pp. 40–41.

2 *The Willowbank Report: Gospel and Culture* (Lausanne Committee for World Evangelization, 1978), p. 14.

3 Ibid., p. 16.

4 Kenneth Cragg, *The Call of the Minaret* (OUP, 1956), pp. 182–183.

5 2 Corinthians 10:1.

6 See e.g. the joint Roman Catholic and World Council study document entitled *Common Witness and Proselytism* (1970).

7 2 Corinthians 13:8.

8 Numbers 16:22; 27:16 (RSV).

9 Genesis 12:2–4.

10 Galatians 3:29.

11 Romans 4:16–17.

12 Galatians 3:8.

13 Psalm 2:8.

14 Psalm 72:11.

15 Isaiah 49:6.

16 Isaiah 2:2.

17 W. G. Blaikie, *David Livingstone* (1908).

18 Matthew 10:6.

19 Matthew 15:24.

20 Matthew 1:2.

21 Matthew 2:1–12.

22 Matthew 8:11.

23 Matthew 28:19–20.

24 Roland Allen, *Pentecost and the World* (OUP, 1917), p. 36.

25 Ibid., p. 40.

26 E.g. Luke 24:49; Acts 1:4, 8.

27 Joel 2:28; Acts 2:17.

28 Acts 8:5–8.

29 Acts 10 and 11.

30 Acts 11:20.

31 Acts 16:6–10.

32 Acts 28:31.

33 Harry R. Boer, *Pentecost and Missions* (Lutterworth, 1961), pp. 161–162.

34 Ibid., p. 217. Query John Stott's, in the original version of *The Contemporary Christian*.

35 Philippians 1:5.

36 2 Thessalonians 3:1.

37 Colossians 4:3.

38 Ephesians 6:19–20.

39 1 Timothy 3:15.

40 1 Peter 2:9.

41 Philippians 2:15–16.

42 1 Thessalonians 1:6, 8.

43 Colossians 4:5–6.

44 1 Peter 3:15.

45 From his address, 'The Enduring Validity of Cross-Cultural Mission', given at the opening of the Overseas Ministries Study Centre's new premises in New Haven, Connecticut, on 5 October 1987, and published in the *International Bulletin of Missionary Research*, April 1988.

46 Revelation 4:1.

47 Revelation 7:9–10.

48 Genesis 13:16.

49 Genesis 15:5.

50 Genesis 22:17.

51 Genesis 13:16 (emphasis added).

52 Genesis 15:5 (emphasis added).

53 Richard Collier, *The General Next to God* (Collins, 1965), p. 146.

3 Holistic mission

1 Raymond Bakke, *Urban Mission*, September 1986, p. 7.

2 Carl F. H. Henry, *Evangelicals at the Brink of Crisis* (Word Books, 1967), pp. 71–72.

3 See R. K. Orchard (ed.), *Witness in Six Continents* (Edinburgh House Press, 1964), p. 157.

4 W. A. Visser 't Hooft, in Norman Goodall (ed.), *The Uppsala 1968 Report* (WCC, 1968).

5 The Lausanne Covenant, para. 5. (John Stott led the team drafting the Lausanne Covenant.)

6 *Evangelism and Social Responsibility: An Evangelical Commitment*, The Grand Rapids Report (Paternoster, 1982), pp. 24–25. (John Stott led the team drafting the report of the Consultation of the Relationship between Evangelism and Social Responsibility.)

7 *The Manila Manifesto: An Elaboration of the Lausanne Covenant 15 Years Later* (Lausanne Committee for World Evangelization, 1989), para. 4, p. 15. (John Stott led the team drafting the Manila Manifesto.)

8 Cf. Galatians 5:6, 13.

9 Cf. Ephesians 2:10 (AV); Titus 2:14.

10 *Evangelism and Social Responsibility*, pp. 21–24.

11 Acts 6:1–7.

12 *Keele '67*, the National Evangelical Anglican Congress Statement, ed. Philip Crowe (Falcon, 1967), para. 2.20, p. 23.

13 John Stott, *Christian Mission in the Modern World* (Falcon, 1975; Kingsway, 1986), pp. 30, 34.

14 John 15:9.

15 John 17:18; 20:21.

16 Deuteronomy 10:12–20.

17 Micah 6:8.

18 1 Kings 18.

19 1 Kings 21.

20 Jeremiah 19:4.

21 Ezekiel 22:3–4; cf. 36:18–19.

22 *Evangelism and Social Responsibility*, p. 20.

23 Mark 6:6 (RSV).

24 Acts 10:38 (RSV).

25 Charles Colson, *Loving God* (Zondervan, 1983), p. 145.

26 Luke 15:11–32.

27 Luke 10:30–37.

28 William Booth, *In Darkest England and the Way Out* (Salvation Army, 1890), p. 14.

29 Ibid., p. 45.

30 Ibid., Preface, p. 4; cf. p. 257.

31 Richard Collier, *The General Next to God* (Collins, 1965), p. 199.

32 John 1:14.

33 J. Herman Bavinck, *An Introduction to the Science of Missions* (1954; ET Presbyterian & Reformed, 1960), p. 113.

34 *The Manila Manifesto*, para. 4: 'The Gospel and Social Responsibility', p. 15.

35 Martin Luther King, in *Strength to Love* (Collins, 1963), p. 34, and in *Stride Toward Freedom: The Montgomery Story* (Harper & Row, 1958), p. 198.

36 From his introduction to *Christian Mission and Social Justice* by Samuel Escobar and John Driver (Herald Press, 1978), pp. 7–9.

37 David Howard, *The Great Commission for Today* (IVP USA, 1976), pp. 84–85.

38 Anne Coomes, *Festa Kivengere: The Authorized Biography* (Monarch, 1990), p. 318.

39 Ibid., p. 455.

40 Ibid., p. 434.

4 The Christology of mission

1 *The Willowbank Report: Gospel and Culture* (Lausanne Committee for World Evangelization, 1978), p. 28.

2 John 17:18; 20:21.

3 1 Corinthians 9:19–22.

4 Richard Collier, *The General Next to God* (Collins, 1965), pp. 91–98.

5 Morris West, *Children of the Sun* (1957; Pan, 1958), especially pp. 82–104.

6 *The Willowbank Report: Gospel and Culture* (Lausanne Committee for World Evangelization, 1978), para. 6(b), p. 18.

7 James Sire, *The Universe Next Door* (IVP, 1976; 2nd edn, 1990).

8 *Your Kingdom Come* (WCC, 1980), p. 143.

9 Lesslie Newbigin, *The Other Side of 1984* (WCC, 1983), especially pp. 22 and 31. See also his *Foolishness to the Greeks* (SPCK, 1986), in which he appeals to us to challenge both 'the scientific worldview' and 'atheistic materialism'.

10 Romans 12:15 (rsv).

11 Isaiah 49:6; cf. 42:1–4.

12 Isaiah 50:6–7.

13 Isaiah 52:15.

14 Isaiah 53:3.

15 Isaiah 53:4–12.

16 Douglas Webster, *Yes to Mission* (SCM Press, 1966), pp. 101–102.

17 John 12:23–24.

18 John 12:26.

19 Ephesians 3:13.

20 2 Timothy 2:10.

21 2 Corinthians 4:12.

22 Richard Collier, *The General Next to God* (Collins, 1965), pp. 104–109.

23 Carolyn Scott, *The Heavenly Witch: The Story of the Maréchale* (Hamish Hamilton, 1981), p. 113.

24 Vincent Donovan, *Christianity Rediscovered: An Epistle from the Masai* (1978; SCM Press, 1982), pp. 193–194.

25 Matthew 28:18–19.

26 E.g. Psalm 86:9.

27 E.g. Isaiah 2:1–3.

28 Johannes Blauw, *The Missionary Nature of the Church* (1962; Eerdmans, 1974), pp. 34, 54, 66. See also Joachim Jeremias, *Jesus' Promise to the Nations* (1956; ET SCM Press, 1958), especially pp. 58–67 which emphasize the centripetal pilgrimage.

29 Ibid., p. 83.

30 Ibid., p. 84.

31 Ibid., p. 166.

32 Ibid., p. 101.

33 Ephesians 1:21 (emphasis added).

34 Philippians 2:9.

35 Colossians 1:18.

36 John Hick and Paul F. Knitter (eds.), *The Myth of Christian Uniqueness* (SCM Press, 1987), p. 20.

37 Philippians 2:9–11.

38 1 Kings 19:10 (RV).

39 2 Corinthians 11:2–3.

40 Constance E. Padwick, *Henry Martyn: Confessor of the Faith* (1922; IVF, 1953), p. 146.

41 Romans 1:5; cf. 3 John 7.

42 Quoted in Gerald H. Anderson and Thomas F. Stransky (eds.), *Christ's Lordship and Religious* Pluralism (Orbis, 1981), pp. 115–117. See also *A Theological Understanding of the Relationship between Christians and Jews*, a paper commended for study by the General Assembly of the Presbyterian Church, USA, in 1987.

43 Quoted by Cormac Murphy-O'Connor, then Bishop of Arundel and Brighton, in *The Family of the Church* (DLT, 1984), p. 41.

44 John R. Mott, *The Decisive Hour of Christian Missions* (Church Missionary Society, 1910), p. 193.

45 John 7:37–39.

46 William Temple, *Readings in St. John's Gospel* (1945; Macmillan, 1955), p. 130.

47 David Wells, *God the Evangelist* (Eerdmans and Paternoster, 1987).

48 *The Manila Manifesto: An Elaboration of the Lausanne Covenant 15 Years Later* (Lausanne Committee for World Evangelization, 1989), para. B.5.

49 See 1 Corinthians 2:1–5; 1 Thessalonians 1:5.

50 The Lausanne Covenant, para. 14.

51 Acts 1:8, 11 (emphasis added).

52 See John Stott, *The Message of Acts* (IVP, 1990), p. 51.

53 Matthew 24:14; cf. Mark 13:10.

54 Lesslie Newbigin, *The Household of God* (SCM Press, 1953), p. 25.

55 2 Corinthians 5:10.

56 2 Corinthians 5:11.

57 Ezekiel 3 and 33.

58 Ezekiel 33:8.

59 2 Timothy 4:1–2.

60 Michael Hennell, *John Venn and the Clapham Sect* (Lutterworth, 1958), p. 245.

Conclusion: the now and the not yet

1 Mark 1:15, as he translates *ēngiken*.

2 Matthew 12:28, *ephthasen*.

3 E.g. Mark 1:14; Matthew 13:16–17.

4 Matthew 12:28–29; cf. Luke 10:17–18.

5 Luke 17:20–21.

6 E.g. Mark 10:15.

7 Matthew 6:10.

8 Matthew 6:33.

9 Mark 9:47; cf. Matthew 8:11.

10 Matthew 25:34.

11 E.g. Isaiah 2:2; Matthew 12:32; Mark 10:30.

12 Galatians 1:4.

13 Colossians 1:13; cf. Acts 26:18; 1 Peter 2:9.

14 Ephesians 2:6; Colossians 3:1.

15 E.g. Matthew 13:39; 28:20.

16 Romans 12:2; 13:11–14; 1 Thessalonians 5:4–8.

17 Romans 8:24; 5:9–10; 13:11.

18 Romans 8:15, 23.

19 John 5:24; 11:25–26; Romans 8:10–11.

20 Psalm 110:1; Ephesians 1:22; Hebrews 2:8.

21 Romans 8:24.

22 Philippians 3:20–21; 1 Thessalonians 1:9–10.

23 Romans 8:19.

24 Romans 8:22–23, 26; 2 Corinthians 5:2, 4.

25 Romans 8:23; 1 Corinthians 1:7.

26 Romans 8:25.

27 E.g. Isaiah 32:15; 44:3; Ezekiel 39:29; Joel 2:28; Mark 1:8; Hebrews 6:4–5.

28 Romans 8:23.

29 2 Corinthians 5:5; Ephesians 1:14.

30 Hebrews 6:4–5.

31 Psalm 119:105.

32 2 Corinthians 5:7.

33 Deuteronomy 34:10; cf. Numbers 12:8; Deuteronomy 3:24.

34 1 Corinthians 13:9–12.

35 Deuteronomy 29:29.

36 1 Thessalonians 4:7–8.

37 Galatians 5:16–26.

38 2 Corinthians 3:18.

39 Galatians 5:17.

40 1 John 1:8.

41 Philippians 3:12–14; 1:6.

42 E.g. Leviticus 19:2.

43 John 8:11 (RSV).

44 E.g. Romans 7:17, 20; 8:9, 11.

45 2 Corinthians 12:12 (RSV).

46 Revelation 11:15.

47 Hebrews 6:5.

48 2 Corinthians 4:10–11.

49 Revelation 21:5.

50 Ephesians 5:27; cf. Revelation 21:2.

51 1 Timothy 6:12.

52 Ephesians 4:3.

53 Matthew 13:30.

54 2 Peter 3:13; Revelation 21:1.

55 Mark 13:7.

56 Isaiah 2:4.

Enjoyed this book? Read the rest of the series.

Presenting John Stott's classic volume in five individual parts for today's audiences, the Contemporary Christian series has been sensitively modernized and updated by Tim Chester but retains the original core, clear and crucial Bible teaching.

The Gospel
978 1 78359 928 8

The Disciple
978 1 78359 930 1

The Bible
978 1 78359 770 3

The Church
978 1 78359 924 0

The World
978 1 78359 926 4